**COLLECTED
EARLY POEMS**

ALSO BY ROBERT LAVETT SMITH

The White Peacock's Throat (1990)
Hesitant Light (1992)
The Nob Hill Mariners (1993)
Jesus In Bed Between Us (1994)
Everything Moves With A Disfigured Grace (2006)
Smoke In Cold Weather (2013)
The Widower Considers Candles (2014)

Sturgeon Moon (2017)

COLLECTED EARLY POEMS

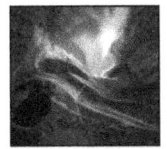

ROBERT LAVETT SMITH

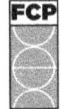

Full Court Press
Englewood Cliffs, New Jersey

First Edition

Copyright © 2018 by Robert Lavett Smith

All rights reserved. No part of this book may be reproduced or
transmitted in any form or by any means electronic
or mechanical, including by photocopying, by recording,
or by any information storage and retrieval system,
without the express permission of the author,
except where permitted by law.

Published in the United States of America
by Full Court Press, 601 Palisade Avenue,
Englewood Cliffs, NJ 07632
fullcourtpress.com

ISBN 978-1-946989-23-9
Library of Congress Catalog No. 2018964865

Editing and book design by Barry Sheinkopf

Author Photo by Laurie Sato

Cover art, "Water Study, Beacon, New York, 2006," by Barry Sheinkopf

FCP Colophon by Liz Sedlack

For Brian, Michael, and Sarah,
*and in gratitude to the many friends and teachers
who showed the way.*

"And the voices,
which once made broken-off, parrot-incoherences,
speak again, this time
speaking on the palatum cordis,
saying there is time, still time
for those who can groan to sing,
for those who can sing to be healed."
—*Galway Kinnell (1927–2014)*

ACKNOWLEDGMENTS

The author wishes to thank the following publications, both in print and online, in which some of these poems first appeared, occasionally in slightly different versions. These include, among others:

Aegis; The Aftermath Press; The Aftermath Press Broadside Series; Anthology One (The Alsop Review); Ball State University Forum; Blue Unicorn; Box of Words; The Clockwatch Review; Curriculum Vitae; The Distillery; The Eckerd College Review; Footprints Magazine; Footwork; The Galley Sail Review; The Granite, 1982; Hanging Loose; Hawai'i Review; The Higginsville Reader; The High Plains Literary Review; The Hiram Poetry Review; Illya's Honey; John Brewer's My Favorite Poems, Part 1; The Journal of New Jersey Poets; The Monkshood Press Broadside Series; Mind Purge; Minotaur; Mudfish; The New Laurel Review; Nightsun; Octavo; Pembroke Magazine; Plainsongs; Pikestaff Forum; Plastic Tower; Poetry Northwest; Potato Eyes; Pudding Magazine; The Raintown Review; Red Owl Magazine; Riverwind; The San Francisco Bay Guardian; Seems; The South Florida Poetry Review; Tar River Poetry; The Tarkington Gazette; The Tomcat; Touchstone; Visions International; Zoo Poems.

The following early chapbooks, long out of print, are reprinted herein in their entirety, with grateful recognition of the original publishers:

The White Peacock's Throat: Feh! Press (1990)
Hesitant Light: Hot Pepper Press (1992)
The Nob Hill Mariners: The Monkshood Press (1993)
Jesus in Bed Between Us: The Tomcat Press (1994)

As always, I would like to thank Barry Sheinkopf for helping me to bring to fruition this, my fifth book, and for his unflagging support and encouragement over what is now nearly forty years. I owe him a debt of gratitude I can never repay.

AUTHOR'S NOTE

As originally conceived, this was to have been my *Collected Poems*, the sum total of my literary career so far. In the course of the past few months, it has become clear that such a project would be cumbersome and impractical at this point, and is in any case premature. At sixty-one I have done a great deal of living, and quite a great deal of writing; still, I dare to hope that much remains ahead for me, and perhaps even that, in the words of a very old song, "the best is yet to come."

I now present, in lieu of the volume I had initially envisioned, my *Collected Early Poems*. The main purpose of this book is to again make available, and in a somewhat more elegant and permanent form, the four long-out-of-print chapbooks which effectively represent the first ten years or so of my poetic output. Many of my earliest poems rank among my best, I think; they still mean a great deal to me. I wanted to rescue them from oblivion. I have included as well some previously unpublished poems from college days; again, I would like to think that they are worth preserving. I have also resuscitated, with minor revisions, my first full-length collection, *Everything Moves With A Disfigured Grace*, which was published years ago by the late Jaimes Alsop, and has become difficult to find.

In the end, selections such as this one always come down to some difficult choices. No doubt I have omitted poems that I ought to have preserved, and preserved others that might best have been consigned to the rubbish. Two poems deliberately appear twice, having evolved into significantly different versions over the years. One or two old favorites are not included simply because I can no longer locate them; perhaps someday they will turn up. In any event, made on a different day, in a different mood, my selection might have been quite different. As my students at the Richmond District's Washington High School never tire of reminding me, "it is what it is."

Robert Lavett Smith,
San Francisco,
September 23, 2018

TABLE OF CONTENTS

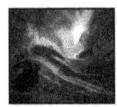

Early Poems, Previously Uncollected (1977–2005)

My Phantom Aunts, *3*
A Rural Staining, *3*
Breviary, *4*
In an Italian Restaurant, *5*
The Glove Tree, *5*
In an Antique Shop, *6*
The Salt Shaker, *7*
Ashtray, *8*
Love Poem, *9*
The Nun's Madhouse, *9*
Morning, *10*
Snow Watch, *11*
The Dragon Robes, *12*
Nocturne for a Woman Nearing Middle Age, *13*
The Dust Storm of April 14, 1935, *14*
A Drunken Italian in a Bar in Milano Tries to Convince Me that I Am Christ, *14*
The Woman and the Orangutan, *15*
Eyes, *16*
She's Sure Her Hands Are on Fire, *16*
Killing the Christmas Fly, *17*
Ancestors, *18*
The Departure, *18*
The Shave, *19*
Walking Alone at Night, *19*
The Book of Artichokes, *20*
Unicorn Soup, *20*

First Frost, 21
She Arrives Just at Dusk, 21

From The White Peacock's Throat (1990)

Greetings from San Francisco, 27
New World, 27
Swimming off Bimini, Summer, 1965, 28
On a Bus at Twilight, 29
Ruth in a Wheelbarrow, 30
Pinocchio, 31
Watching Marguerite, 32
The Visitors, 33
Portrait of a Lady, 34
An Old Man with an Easel, 35
Visiting the Undertaker, 35
Cross of Nails, 38
The Verrazano Narrows at a Distance, 38
A Smell like Ashes, Guam, 1949, 40
Paestum, 40
Thirty Years after the War, 40
The Embarkation, 42
Driving South from San Francisco, 42
Elegy for a Spanish Poet, 43
Requiem, 44
The Pogo Stick, 45
The Ghost in the Basilica, 46
Why the French Seldom Eat Corn, 47
The Windows, 48
Attending the Bishop's Mass, 49
Loss, 49
History Rises, 50
In Memory of Weldon Kees, 51
Even So, 52

What the Eye Is Drawn To, 53
The Stars, 54
The Seasons of a Year, 55
Omens and Portents, 55
The Death This Year, 56
The Werewolf's Grave, 57
Sultan School for Handicapped Children, 58
Crosses Made of Flowers, 58
Dinner with Lisa, 59
Falling out of Love at the Columbus Zoo, 60
Saint Jerome and the Skull, 61
Waiting for the Thaw, 61
Family Chronicle, 62
Walking beside the Hudson, 63
The Bo Tree, 65
Some Kind of Permanence, 66
The White Peacock's Throat, 67

From Hesitant Light (1992)

Sunday Morning, Early: The Richmond, San Francisco, 71
A Palmistry, 71
An Afternoon by the Carousel, 72
Self Portrait at 34: On the Golden Gate Bridge, 72
Spring: Two Views, 73
At the Fundamentalist Church, 74
In Memory of a Failed Messiah, 75
Jesus, 75
Pictures of the Dead, 76
New Year's Day: The Sutro Baths, 77
San Francisco, My Thirty-Fourth Year, 77
Dreaming of Aftershocks, 78
The Bodies of Bonnie and Clyde, 78
Illinois Wedding, 79

The Wedding Photographs of Strangers, *79*
The Appian Way, 1974, *80*
My Father Emerges from the Depths, *81*
Our High School Choir Performs at a Black Church, *82*
Paterson, *82*
Twilight, *Crème Caramel*, and a Woman Named Shawn, *83*
I Die, *83*
The Rooms We Live In, *84*
A Basket of Silk Flowers, *84*
The Death of Willie Dixon: As Reported on National Public Radio, January 29, 1992, *85*
At a Civil War Reenactment, *86*
The Bridge, Soon Afterwards, *87*
The Blue Angels Pass Overhead, *87*
At Bean Hollow, *88*

From The Nob Hill Mariners (1994)

The Nob Hill Mariners, *93*
A Letter to Meg in New York, *93*
A Nocturne for Fisherman's Wharf, *94*
From the 41st Floor, *95*
Dana's Pipe, *95*
For the Builder of Golden Gate Park, *97*
Snow in the Berkeley Hills, *98*
Terri Arranges the Mantelpiece, *99*
Goldilocks, *99*
The Importance of Space, *100*
The Slow Loris, *101*
Sand Dollars, *102*
The Bottlebrush Plant, *103*
Driving Past, *104*
A Tricycle Abandoned on the Sidewalk after Dark, *104*
Fog on Ocean Beach, *104*

The Brandenburg Concerti, *105*
Bad Fruit, *107*
Rain Offshore, *107*
Simply Being Here, *108*

From Jesus In Bed Between Us (1994)

Among Believers, *111*
Chinatown in Fog, *111*
Earthquake Weather, *112*
Light and Darkness, *113*
Meatloaf, *114*
October Moon, Nearly Full, through Clouds, *114*
Pebbles from a Northern Field, *115*
Three Northern California Landscapes, *116*
Jesus in Bed between Us, *117*
The Morning Mail, *117*
The Scrapbook, *118*
The Blind Clarinet Player, *119*
Nicollet in Wisconsin, 1639, *119*
My Father Takes Me Fishing, *120*
I Celebrate Five Years in San Francisco: October 6, 1992, *121*
East of Modesto, *122*
Beyond Radio Range, *122*
An African Carving, *123*
A Decorative Mantelpiece from Early in the Century, *124*
Buxtehude by Candlelight, *124*
Wedding: The Annunciation Greek Orthodox Church, Modesto, *125*
A Half-Empty Pack of Cigarettes, *126*
A Vietnamese Grass Beverage: Three Poems, *127*

Curios, from Sturgeon Moon (2017)

The Wedding, *131*
Lullaby and Dirge, *132*

Scène de Genre, 133
Apple Trees, 133
Answering the Riddle, 134
Primer, 135
The Peacemakers, 136
Audley End, 136
Hearses, 137
Nocturne, 138
Watching a Blind Man in a Subway Station, 139
Knife Grinder, 139
The Unfinished Throne, 140
The Flower Burning, 141
Dance of the Dresses, 142
If I Had My Druthers, 143

Everything Moves With A Disfigured Grace (2006)

The Skull of Billy the Kid, 149
The Final Hours of the Twentieth Century, 150
From One Who Has No Right to Grieve, 150
My Grandfather's Vigil, 151
The Clockwork Farm, 152
Landscape with Figure, Standing Apart, 153
Deaf Woman Wrapping Christmas Gifts at Borders, 154
Dust Bowl Funeral, 154
Gardening along the Fire Scars: Oakland, 1993, 155
Don't Look Now, 156
In the Name of Science, 156
After Brain Surgery, 157
Classical Musicians in the Subway, 158
Kickballs, 158
Brie and Chianti at Midnight, 159
At Last, like Sleepers, 159
Bob Dylan Is Stopped by His Own Security, 160
The Trouble with the Garage Sale, 160

Dreaming in Black and White, *161*
Etta and the Seagulls, *162*
Little Elegy, *163*
Chinese New Year, the Bowery, *167*
Crossing Larkspur Ferry, *167*
Night Braces, *168*
The Cathedral, *169*
The Partial Hospitalization Unit, *170*
The Onset of Something Ominous, *171*
A Lament for My Forty-Fourth Year, *172*
Catechism for a Leper, *172*
The Truest World, *173*
Ciro on the Night before His Wedding, *174*
The Nuns' Madhouse, *175*
The Ceremony, *175*
The Last Shakers of Sabbathday Lake, *176*
Nothing I Love Has Ever Seemed Permanent, *177*
Terrors of the Millennium, *177*
Walking across the Sea of Galilee, *178*
Sunrise, San Francisco, September 1, 1999, *179*
Morning Meditation, *180*
The Yellow House in Arles, *181*
Elegy Which Should Have Been a Blues, *182*
In Response to a Prediction of My Death on April 4, 2031, *182*
Who Wants to Be an Impoverished Poet?, *183*
Electrocuting the Elephant, *187*
The Ordinary Arrival of Death, *188*
Droppings, *188*
The Dolls, *189*
A Street at the End of the World, *190*
Watching the Tall Ships, *190*
Einstein the Watchmaker, *192*
Cockatoo and Cockroaches, *193*
Maxfield Parrish, *194*

The Squirrels, *195*
For Geoffrey Hill, *196*
The Day They Closed the Mustang Ranch, *196*
Snow on the Colorado Plains, *197*
The Songwriter Addresses His Fans, *198*
Bell Choir, *198*
A Cyanide Lake in an Old Mining Town, *199*
Expulsion from the Garden, *199*
At Your Bedside, *200*
In the Shadow of the Reaper, *200*
Flamingoes in the Camargue, *201*
Peppermint Pig, *201*

Index of Titles, 203
About the Author, 211

EARLY POEMS
Previously Uncollected
(1977–2005)

MY PHANTOM AUNTS

A surprise to see them
though I know they're kin.

They arrive together,
bonneted, in black.
Pinched faces vague
as old tintypes.

As usual, they politely
decline my offered tea.
Perched on chairs
passed through six wars,
gossip of outlaws, injuns
and whiskey-swilling preachers
in faint, pleasant voices.

Moonlight falls through
the folds of dark calico.
They really are charming,
if a bit stiff and proper.

When they leave at dawn
I've promised to visit.

A RURAL STAINING

*They would take soft soap,
mix the black with it, and
stain the coffin while the
men would be telling their
merry stories.*

If he owned no boards
split the wood yourself.

Fill the death room
with the noise of hammers
while candles shiver
above his head.

Tell stories as you work.
About the winter the river froze
and men made fires on the ice,
fishing for three days and nights.
About the giant's tooth they found
at last spring's plowing.

When every joint fits snug
rub the grain with soap,
lampblack diluted with whiskey.
Watch how the bright pine
drinks darkness from your fingers
in wide, uneven swaths.

BREVIARY

You're praying the same old prayers
again, the ones
where no god intrudes.

Coffee, black. Two eggs
over easy. You claim
you don't believe in ritual.

Ruth's chair is empty.
You set two places
out of habit. Strawberries
because she liked them.

Between mouthfuls
you parrot words:

crabgrass, antifreeze.
Notice the spigot's windy dripping.

Nights, she sleeps beside you;
absent hands
knead your heart's bread.

IN AN ITALIAN RESTAURANT

A missionary girl
goes from table to table
selling postcards.

Even as she smiles
and hands them to you,
you start to see them in her eyes.

First the blind virgin
drawing water from an empty stream,
blessing a cupful of dust.

Then the wounded stag,
horns like dark branches.
The hounds whose teeth
leave a hot script in his side.

Suddenly, you see yourself—
upturned face startled
like a coin in a beggar's palm.

THE GLOVE TREE

*In Puritan New England, gloves were
sent as invitations to funerals.*

Almost before you could walk,
you walked to the graveyard.

Lay spread-eagled like an angel
on a grave your size, piled earth

still damp and bare. Your father
nodded approvingly, his shadow

covering you. At night in dreams
you returned alone, to wander

through high grass, among stony
swollen breasts and gawking skulls.

Even in winter, one tree was never
bare. Its broad, leathery leaves

rattled like distant laughter,
or the windy creek of reeds.

IN AN ANTIQUE SHOP

The room seems brown at the corners,
like an old print. There are candlesticks
on a carved table, and ice-pale goblets

bright as lilies. "Scenes From The Hunt"
line one wall, in heavy frames.
Dogs pull at the carcass; a horse

crops grass the color of old ivory.
Men clean flintlocks, while we
imagine brocaded coats are red, wigs

chalk-white with powder. No pigment's left
after so long, only a hint of ocher and ash—
barely enough to darken the piled clouds.

The living circulate, nodding curiously.
Round and smooth, a child's pink fingers
shine in the dim light, as he rides

his father's shoulders through the clutter
of walnut, green brass, and dust.
They come to the water-stained "Hunt."

Horse, says the father, lips wrinkling
to a smile. *Horse*, repeats the child,
the word new and strange in his mouth.

THE SALT SHAKER

Glancing back,
she sees the city
turn to smoke.

Her husband plods on
resolutely,
into his grief.

Startled
in her glass gown,
she graces

tables where we
break bread
for long journeys.

We taste
her tears,
now dry as dust.

ASHTRAY

For Connie

It keeps filling
up with stars.

Nobody knows why.

The sky at any rate
isn't any emptier.

Still the bright powder
burns and darkens:
there seems to be
no end to it.

As for the ashtray itself,
it is glass.
There are many stories
concerning its birth.

Some say it grew
from a glass bead
carelessly dropped
in an open furrow.

Most believe
it was spit burning
from a volcano,
and fell into the sea
like a tektite.

For a while,
it was considered sacred.
It shone in the nave
like a marble font,

or a priest's upturned palm.

All we know
of it for sure
is that it keeps

filling up
with stars.

LOVE POEM

He keeps writing
Sara, Sara
on a piece of paper.
He's alone in his little room,
sitting at a desk:
the moon floats like a worn coin
in his window.

Odd, he thinks,
how the moon changes hands.

Now the paper is a field,
ragged with pale grass.
A name keeps disappearing into it—
like a road
where no one walks.

THE NUN'S MADHOUSE

> "He heard a mad nun screeching in the nuns' madhouse
> beyond the wall."
> —James Joyce

Here, the darkness cupped between praying hands
is released, to quiver
like a dark flame in the painted eyes

of a plaster Christ who hangs
lopsided on a pine cross.
His body is a fleshy sail
drooping on its mast,
adrift on the wall's greasy whiteness.
Ancient women who beg for nothing,
not even grace, grind the beads of endless days
in veined hands, brown teeth chattering,
chattering. One drools listlessly
onto her threadbare habit;
a jagged stain spreads on the black cloth.
Jesus, says another, Jesus:
a name the years
have softened to sobbing.

At night the whiteness dims:
hoarse prayers rise like crows
to hover about the crucifix.
The broken psalms of praise
are the hardest to forget.
When the sun falls in wide red stripes
through the window grates,
nurses bring the moist smell of soup
to their sisters pinned to earth
by the shadow of the cross.

—1982 version

MORNING

Wives skim the cream
off frozen bottles.
Horse-lime steams in the street.
A wet sweet smell of melons
hangs like a halo
over the sagging brown awning
of Rafferty's market.

The sky is smeared with smoke;
on the river, sails swell
against the bridge with its damp web
of wires. As the rows
of wooden storefronts redden
and fill with color,
a stray mongrel sniffs and paws
at drunks huddled in doorways.
Their eyes are rolled upward
out of the light
like the marble eyes
of Roman statues.

SNOW WATCH

I am expecting snow tonight.
Don't really care that it's July.
Have been lugging this weather

around all week. In the street
below my window mist rises in strands
as if an old woman braided her hair

by moonlight. Streetlights bloom
on their stalks. I wonder if she thinks of
love, weaving her ropes of rainy dust?

Easy now to imagine this town
dimming to whiteness, edge of every roof
softening. In the streetlight beam

the rising mist sharpens to flakes,
tumbles back, cold, thick as milkweed
fluff. A bother, really. Next morning

the grass is brittle, shrunken with summer.
Certain the snow is hiding somewhere,
I search the lawn for icy prints.

THE DRAGON ROBES

> *In 1638 an explorer, Jean Nicollet, carried mandarin robes
> with him into the Wisconsin wilderness.*

Light slants through the birch leaves
onto the folded robes. Their silk rocks brightly
in the palm of a pale canoe.

His beard has lengthened in the wilderness.
He stares at himself from the broad, wrinkled river:
hair fanned out in an alien dawn

like the halo of a biblical sage.
A firm flesh ripples beneath his buckskins;
his eyes grow dark and hard

in leathery cheeks. The rifle's crack
rings in his veins until it becomes
part of the stillness, like the quick swish of arrows

finding their mark. He cuts spearheads and fishhooks
from antler-bone. Speaks less and less
with the native guides: lithe red men

with stony, expressionless faces.
They carry the shining Cathay silks
up the Saint Lawrence, banks thick with trees;

flies whir and sparkle all around.
Nicollet dreams of the Khan,
picturing spires of lace and ivory

rising in Wisconsin under a ripe,
golden sun. At last, alerted by scouts,
he strides onto the soft brown plain

like Christ over still water. A thin smoke
mounts from a circle of ragged wigwams
to hang in the dazed afternoon. Lightning slices

across the cold blue of his Bourbon eyes—
half-naked savages squat in the dust,
picking lice from beaver pelts. The useless robes,

vivid with dragons and lotus blossoms,
float in the blackness of their startled gaze,
above the flat, indifferent grassland.

—1982 version

NOCTURNE FOR A WOMAN NEARING MIDDLE AGE

Nowadays she only knows
which of her daughters is home
by which car is in the driveway.
At night, the pale beams
of headlights stretch through drawn curtains
to step across the darkness where her husband's
slow breath marks the minutes
until morning. She hears an engine roll over
outside; the younger girl's laughter
like a shower of glass stars.
A key turns in the lock
with a dry click; the hinges whisper hoarsely
to the silent hallway. The even pad of footsteps
climbs like a heartbeat
up the unlit stairs.

THE DUST STORM
OF APRIL 14, 1935

*Taken from conversations with Woody
Guthrie recorded during the 1940s.*

It came in off the plains,
so black you couldn't tell what it was.
Even the old timers, some who'd lived
in town fifty years or more,
had never seen anything like that.
It was like night fell
all of a sudden at noontime.
Folks all crowded into their houses,
hands before their faces.
Light bulbs left only
red inchworms of light.
The old folks said, well, they figured this was it.
There'd be a darker river
to cross soon. And the dust rippled
across the floor like water,
covering tables and chairs.
Plows crumbled to rust,
weathercocks staggered in the gritty breeze.

A DRUNKEN ITALIAN IN A BAR IN MILANO TRIES TO CONVINCE ME THAT I AM CHRIST

Dark hands gesture excitedly:
Jesus Christ, you!

There *is* the beard.
The way I sleep at night,
arms spread like a stripped

scarecrow.

But no, he is mistaken.
I set my empty glass on the counter,
clots of purple blood
dripping from punctured wrists.

In the street, commotion.
Everyone barters for each other's clothes.
We stone one another
with fistfuls of coins,
the mossy rubble of churches.

THE WOMAN AND THE ORANGUTAN

A naked woman has
been kissed by an orangutan.

No doubt an honest mistake.

It happened in Borneo.
They have
naked women there.

The woman, named Mautama,
had been bathing
in the thick brown river
which runs by her village.

Climbing out
to sun herself on a rock,
she felt the long, hairy arms
reach for her,
and was startled.

Now she seldom speaks,
and refuses the rice
her husband brings
in a little mahogany bowl.

At night when he touches her,
she pushes him away.

The rising moon
above the banyan trees
puckers,
becoming a pair
of wide, leathery lips.

EYES

Someone said it's the eyes remain. Cheeks sag and darken; our eyes drift through time like candles an old Slavic woman sends downstream, bearing prayers for her dead. They lodge in faces everyday a little more like stone. Then there's the dark angel grinning in old woodcuts: sockets into which life swirls like dim water. Grandfathers in starched collars who stare from the silvery torpor of tintypes, eyes mute with dust. Finally, blind eyes, to which the salt of drowning clings, even in bus stations, supermarkets.

SHE'S SURE HER HANDS ARE ON FIRE

For Karen Propp

Since she was seven
she's been convinced
her hands are on fire.
She's amazed
that no one seems to notice.

Her father always told her
to wash them well.
She wonders why the water
doesn't put them out.
On buses she's embarrassed
by the smoke.
None of the other passengers
look up from their papers.
She buys a plastic raincoat
with large pockets,
never wears it
for fear it may melt.
At last she decides
to consult a specialist,
wonders why the phone
feels cool to her touch.
The doctor leans back
in his overstuffed chair,
scribbles on a pad.
The tips of his fingers
glow like blown glass.

KILLING THE CHRISTMAS FLY

*It is bad luck ever to
kill a Christmas fly.*

Happens so fast
you hardly know.
On the lace tablecloth
hair-legs
twitch in a speck of blood.
Already the sky
dims,
mirrors shiver
in their oaken frames.
Father, with
horn-handled knife,

mother, pouring wine,
don't notice.
The cat
sits up suddenly,
ears pricked.
It's as if
a high-pitched whine
fills the far corners
of the room.
A summer sound,
air shagged with ice.
Darkness
in the pale of the year.

ANCESTORS

Searching the family album
I regret to report
no sign of werewolves,
and nobody burned at the stake.

But I do boast some Indian blood—
I can tell by the shape of my teeth.

There's a great uncle somewhere
who drank himself to death
when the distillery train derailed.

And a whole lot of aunts
who hushed such matters up.

THE DEPARTURE

All afternoon
the shadows have been deepening
in the still country of your face.

For a moment I thought
I could see your hand move
beneath the blankets.

Now you are only the wind
stirring in the yard below.

I lower the shade
just as the sun
turns the windows
of the tenements
to fire.

THE SHAVE

For Charles Simic

Remarkable how clearly I recall
the Italian barber shop
smelling of warm towels
and aftershave.

The way my eyes followed a crack
in the high molded ceiling
as if volumes were written
in its sinuous unwinding.

The cold blade of a straight razor
rounding the curve of my cheek,
its touch as vivid to me now
as the touch of a woman once loved.

WALKING ALONE AT NIGHT

For Louis Grace

The stars shine more brightly here
than they ever do above cities.

They are like words of a language so old
the sky itself has forgotten.

THE BOOK OF ARTICHOKES

It came to pass that Ozymandias ordered his slaves to construct an artichoke, as a tomb for his favorite wife. The royal architect wrinkled his dark Ethiopian brow, then shook his head. No one had ever seen an artichoke; no one even knew for sure what they looked like. Before long, however, great carts of lapis lazuli arrived from lands with strange names; from every corner of the realm, merchants brought fistfuls of sapphires. In the smithies of Ur and Babylon, vast sheets of copper were beaten into broad, red leaves. But the wise men murmured in their beards: They could not agree on the blueprint. Eventually, all work was shut down, although the king's craftsmen had completed only a single ornament—a strange, coppery flower meant to grace the artichoke's broad dome. The leaves are green now, with age, but are still stiff, and hold their shape.

UNICORN SOUP

Once upon a time, there was a bowl of unicorn soup, on special that Tuesday at the best restaurant in town. There it sat, on the white linen tablecloth, in a low porcelain bowl, with a container of grated cheese to sprinkle on top, if the customer wanted any. There were croutons, too. "And *how* do I know this is unicorn soup?" asked the customer, tucking his soft, bleached napkin into his collar. The *maître d'* just stood there frowning, with a towel over his arm. The customer dipped his silver spoon into the unicorn soup, and raised a spoonful to his lips. There in the spoon, letters were forming into a very old story, about a farm from his childhood: a collie dog, and a barn with moss-green walls. In the street outside the restaurant, the snow got deeper and deeper, filling up everyone's footprints.

FIRST FROST

Past sixty, I hear more clearly now than ever
my own footsteps ringing in the hollow of my skull.
Words written years ago come back to taunt me
like the voice of a stranger in a childish dream.

Once, I lay watching as the shadow
of your hair brushed your sleeping face;
your lashes were dark moons
risen and lovely in a pale sky.

As if I believed that sort of thing these days.
Sadness seems frozen to my life,
like frost on a windowpane.
The coming winter will be long and deep.

—Written spring, 1987; revised June 21, 2018

SHE ARRIVES JUST AT DUSK

The February wind
rattles the windows,
and she stands in front of them
framed by the falling night.

Behind her glasses her eyes
are trembling light;
her knuckles whiten
around her purse strap.

When she speaks
a silence lingers
like winter starlight
on her lips.

Long after she has gone
I will continue to picture her
walking alone down black streets
quivering with rain.

POEMS FROM THE CHAPBOOKS
(1990–1994)

From *The White
Peacock's Throat*
(1990)

In memory of Joan Yarns

GREETINGS FROM SAN FRANCISCO

How like ourselves they are,
these griefs doing their slow shuffle
through all the places where we outgrew them,
as familiar as our worn-out clothes.
On Fisherman's Wharf, for instance,
it's midsummer,
the sky scalded and ready to crack.
The prison throbs like a scar on the bay,
its iron rooms vacant but for wind.

We walk for hours along the water,
breathing the heaviness of decay.
The long streets smell of sunlight.
Friendship, at such moments,
is a shared uneasiness,
and love, a hollowness
nothing seems to cure.
On Lombard Street hydrangeas quiver
as though a hand had brushed them and drawn back.

NEW WORLD

*"Concerning Lions, I will not say
that I ever saw any myself."*
—William Wood, New England's Prospect, 1639

It wasn't the Eden we'd thought.

We arrived in the dead of winter:
ponds and streams were clogged with ice.

That spring, the soil brought forth
stones, and sharp hooks of yellow bone.

Some said these were Satan's teeth,
and prayed fervently. Lions were heard

in the black underbrush within a mile
of Plimouth. Their howling surprised us

at prayer: the pale wings of open Bibles
beat in our hands. Hymns rose like smoke.

SWIMMING OFF BIMINI, SUMMER, 1965

Jellyfish
swell and rot
in the shallows,
having drifted
too close to shore.
Farther out,
the water
is nearly black,
shards of sunlight
splintering just
below the surface.
Even at the ripe
old age of eight
I can't swim
well enough
to go out
that far,
but my father
takes me
on his back
to see the reef,
my face mask
too large

and leaking.

Someday I will wonder
if death is like this.

In a silent forest
of sea fans,
glittering fish
dart around us
with acrobatic ease,
a whirl of knives
shredding blue light.
Language is
useless now.
We are weightless
and mute,
our own breath
shining above us
like glass.

ON A BUS AT TWILIGHT

It's years ago,
and the hour just after sunset
when substance bleeds into shadow.
Through the tinted window
of a bus bound for somewhere I don't remember,
a broken smokestack passes
at the highway's edge—
black marshes stirring beyond,
the sky already threadbare
with the first stars.

My loneliness complete,
I can look unafraid

into the lives of strangers:
the old men warming their hands
over an ashcan,
or the girl whose long hair,
seen for an instant through yellow curtains,
falls in a dark cascade
through the barber's scissors
into the lost and perfect light.

RUTH IN A WHEELBARROW

Coming unexpectedly across your photograph,
I wonder again whether you're dead,
killed by the drugs and the foreign lovers,
by waiting table and cleaning toilets,
by the thin sorrow in your voice
on the phone from Omaha at midnight,
years ago.

The winter we met in France
we sat for hours in filthy cafés
while you talked of your father's new wife
or the latest Spaniard you'd been to bed with,
and the light from the lamps
crackled in the cellophane from your cigarette wrapper
or settled like oil
onto our beer.

In a letter some time later
you sent me this one picture.
You had recently come from El Salvador,
where the streets were swollen with corpses
and your lover had left you for a man.
Back in the states now,
you had no steady job

and slept where you could.
You were barely nineteen.

It's been too long
since your last letter.
All that remains of you
is the immense poverty
of a summer dawn
when the sky was a thin gauze
the light had worn through.
You sit in a wheelbarrow
behind a faintly shining
white farmhouse
which seems too quaint to be real,
wind tangled through
your loose brown hair.
Cabbages brood around you
like deep black roses.
The last stars
fade in your eyes.

PINOCCHIO

In one old drawing
the newly enlivened puppet
dances with his arms outspread,
half in the stance of the marionette—
although we see no strings—
half in grotesque imitation

of a crucified Christ.
The nails protruding at his wrists
intensify our sense that this carved flesh,
though not yet human, hums
with human pain, the grain of the wood

beneath his paint
tightening to muscle,
beginning to bleed.

The high cheekbones and long clown nose
the carver's chisel gave him
lend his painted face the exaggerated
gaiety of a child's nightmare,
some feverish dream
that marries wood and blood.
But as a child,

I loved this book more than any other:
the steel leg braces
which held my disobedient
limbs in place
made me feel puppet-like,
each awkward step constrained as though by wires;
and even very young I understood

the agony behind that varnished smile—
the longing, perpetually deferred,
for stiffened flesh to be made real;
the striving of the nearly-human
to finally be unremarkable:
supple and warm as anyone,
freed of nails, freed of strings.

WATCHING MARGUERITE

Studying your face
I am reminded
of the frayed
sad faces
of courtly lovers

in old tapestries,
whose eyes,
undimmed by centuries,
betray no pity
for the weakness
of the heart;
it startles me to feel
so great an aching
at your every gesture—
the way you light a cigarette,
or stand at the sink dicing carrots
while your hair buries the light.

THE VISITORS

Tonight the darkness
finds the door again
and enters without knocking.

Now the dead,
blinded and bodiless,
hover here like friends—
repeating to themselves
the words they've said
through twenty or a hundred lifetimes,
their tongues edged with a fire
fainter than starlight.

They gather lives
like half-remembered songs,
old melodies they never
quite get right.

And entering our dreams
they reinvent the past:

What river is this,
what garden,
what copper sunlight
falling through the trees?

PORTRAIT OF A LADY

"Ma coupe est pleine."
—Carmen Lluch, 1978

The image that always returns
is of the room in Paris
with the shutters drawn,
late afternoon sun
falling in crooked stripes
through the louvers,
and your face
adrift in white hair.
I remember the cheap phonograph
and the one scratchy record
of bird calls,
the voices of starlings
filling the silences in our talk,
the way your hands trembled
as you served tea.
But is it true as you claimed
that you once taught school in Valencia,
while the city burned around you?
Or that twice
you put your head in the oven,
but each time
the landlady found you in time?
And why did you always wear those dark glasses,
even indoors—
as though you were blind,
or afraid of the light?

AN OLD MAN WITH AN EASEL

For Claude Monet

The garden is dark now
even at noon.
Wide leaves clog the pond,
edged with vermilion;
wind rattles the slats
of the Japanese bridge.
Hunched in his greatcoat
he paints from memory,
feeling the sun
on the back of his hand.

VISITING THE UNDERTAKER

1.
On afternoons like this
his eighty-two years come back,
lurching through the distance
like the Model T's he used to use for hearses.

How immense and firm he seems
seated in his shapeless chair
here in the house he built when he was young—
the light like woven silk behind him,
his sinewed limbs as stony as the graves
farmhands dug by hand before the war
for fifty cents a day.

Trade embalmer,
he calls himself with pride,
his grin all real teeth
beneath a fringe of silver hair
which glows on his brow.
He worked for morticians
in three states

and remembers it all:
breaking the jaws of stunned, still faces
to force them into a smile;
the blood-blued alcohol
which turned the chalkiness of death
into an innocence like sleep;
how, in the thirties, the milkman
coming by horse from the outlying farms
would knock on his door at dawn
to announce another passing.

2.
During the Depression
people kept dying,
so business was good—
apart from a rumor he never verified
that some of his colleagues
dug up new graves after dark
to use the coffin and the tux again.
He married, and is still amazed
at how his wedding photographs resemble
a lifetime spent at funerals.
He led the Independence Day parade
in a crisp new fireman's uniform,
his arms scalded by a garland of roses.

All in all, he prospered, although
the Tuesday night poker games
at the Masonic Lodge
were played with cards worn dull with use;
although he and his sons would bounce nickels
on his grandmother's marble-topped table
to be sure they were real.

3.
His was a business like any other,
even when it came to burying kinfolk.
The only mortician for seventy miles,

he had to do the job himself.
It amazes him that he felt nothing,
arranging friends he'd known since childhood
under the shine of coffin sheets.
But when his wife of sixty years passed on
he chose the crepe dress from the bedroom closet—
threading his way through a wilderness of shoes—
then phoned a fella he'd worked for in New York.
Some things a man must leave to strangers.

4.
If his dreams are ever troubled
by all the eyes whose glassy stare he weathered
until he pressed the lids over them,
he never says so—
except to note in passing that the dead
seem lighter somehow than the living do;
their limbs are cold, of course,
but full of air,
as though some burden had been lifted from them.
They powdered underneath his touch like dust.

He knows death well, but won't
talk of it for very long.
Instead he points
to the windowsill
where two antique bottles
found near the railroad tracks
have turned violet
from decades of sunlight.
Old glass has colors in it
it may take years to see.
His voice is steady, his gaze
clear and unafraid.
The light, he says, *the light—*
it changes everything.

CROSS OF NAILS
For Michael De Porte

It was summer when we visited
Coventry. Boughs fragrant
with apple blossoms crowded
through the windows
of the bombed
cathedral. The roof
was open to the sky.
A cross made from nails
rescued from the ruin
stood on the altar,
disfigured by damp petals
just as, in winter,
it must have been
by snow. Sunlight
lay like silk
on everything.
We didn't believe the guides
who told us
of other crosses
which fell through the air,
singing as they came.

THE VERRAZANO NARROWS AT A DISTANCE

Through the haze I can see
the dully gleaming span,
and a dark knot of gulls
tying and untying itself
in the air.
It's cold for late March,
silent as only
Sunday morning can be.

I'm sitting alone
at the Castle Point lookout
where the only sound
is the rope banging
hollowly against the flagpole,
feeling the chill
of the marble bench
through my jeans.
And as is true
every time I come here,
I can't help but imagine
my own body broken and bloodied
on the rocks below—
a bent, still spot
beside the shining water.
Although my life seems blessed
now that the wind tastes of spring,
I contemplate death
with the kind of dull wonder
that makes a man holding a knife
feel compelled to run his finger
along the cutting edge.
There is, after all,
nothing in myself
that the world would really miss
were I to take that dizzying step
into oblivion.
But I always remember the bridge:
the way it seems incredibly
to hang in the void—
supported by nothing,
as the heart is—
how, like the heart,
it carries us bravely
between one thing
and the next.

—Hoboken, 1985

A SMELL LIKE ASHES, GUAM, 1949

In the days
just after the war,
they often dug
unexploded bombs
out of the unpaved
village streets,
and whole towns held their breath
while corroded landmines were rowed
out past the reef and dumped overboard,
churning the green water white
and leaving the tartness of ashes
to hang in the air for hours.
In some coastal areas
old women still wash
that smell from their hair
on afternoons swollen with storms.
They speak in whispers
and keep a vigil for the dead.

PAESTUM
i.m. Helen A. Gulemarian, 1933--2017

The sea goes on ringing its bronze bells.
Good land is so scarce the dead are buried standing up.
Eyeless legions march under the earth
while the wind above them
hones its knives on broken columns.

THIRTY YEARS AFTER THE WAR
Palau, 1971

The thatch has nearly worn away
from the roof of the meeting house

where the guide shows me
the silhouettes of aircraft
carved into a storyboard
with the rising sun of Japan
on their wings.

But this is not an island that remembers,
although one still finds sometimes
the green copper casing of a machine gun shell
half-buried in the sand
near the water's edge.
The leaves of the coconut palms
lull the mind with their indolent rhythm,
and the unblinking eye of the sea—
so clear you can count the stripes
on a lion fish thirty feet below—
is almost never darkened by storms.

So things continue pretty much as usual.
A local shopkeeper keeps the skull
of a Japanese soldier as a trophy
on a shelf, between cans of whale meat
and ribbons of dried cod,
but nowadays he hardly ever
takes it down for tourists.

As our jeep turns onto the main road,
heading back to Koror,
we pass a gang of convicts
digging a ditch.
Bare-breasted women with flowers in their hair
smile and wave
from beneath a rust-streaked porch
of corrugated iron.

In the cemetery
men in traditional mourning blue

are folding the flag from the coffin
of a boy home from Vietnam.

THE EMBARKATION

The faces of the dead
in their mahogany boxes
are always fish-like: colorless skin
pulled tightly over their cheeks,
the nearly invisible
breathless lines of their lips.
Flowers encircle them
like splintered sea foam.

The living nod sadly.
Nobody watches as the dark boats
sink slowly
into the earth.

DRIVING SOUTH
FROM SAN FRANCISCO

The morning pulls like a stitch
from an old wound.
Sunlight rots the blond hills.
The cypresses are palsied
by the wind which moves like memory
over the highways,
through filling stations
unpainted since the fifties,
where flags snap
and laundry sours in the heavy air,
miles from the sea.

From out of nowhere a brown moth,

shaking dust from its wings,
twitches against the windshield
and vanishes:
tentative as longing,
brief as love.
Their bodies gone, the dead stumble
out of the Dust Bowl and the gold rush
in their rotten shoes,
casting no shadows
as they turn bewildered
towards the end
of another century.

ELEGY FOR A SPANISH POET

It's one of those brown countries
with narrow streets and iron balconies
from which girls throw flowers.
Today is bull-running day
and somehow you're floating
above the crowds, the runners, and the bull
whose broad back is ribboned with blood
as though he has been broken for a fight,
the spikes they used to goad him
thrust through his flesh like quills,
an orchid twisted around each one.

You drift over roofs caked with pigeon droppings
into a sky so blue it burns.
Your death is the bull's,
far below—
his collapsed form
a stain on the pavement,
swollen in the sun.
In the marketplace,
a miniature funeral is passing,

mourners like sad black ants
carrying a matchbox coffin.
The corpse is carved of ice.

You can move where you wish, unseen,
barely more than a breath of wind.
Darkness is falling,
and from the street beneath you
accordion music uncurls
through a lanterned dusk.

REQUIEM

i.m. D.S.W., 1924–1975

It's more than ten years
since a friend brought me
the news of your death
as I drank stale coffee
in an all-night diner,
and I still grieve sometimes—
although I have no right to,
since we were almost strangers.

The ghost
of your last heartbeat
still shudders
like lightning
across my memory,
bringing back
those days of corridors
and hospital shelves
where your blood glowed
in long rows of vials
arranged as precisely
as votives.

Nothing here
has changed.
Those who loved you
love you still.
Our days now
are as brittle
as old skin,
like hollow footfalls
on a broken stair.

THE POGO STICK
For Charles Simic

Once, late at night,
as I walked homeward
down a desperate street
where the stores were all shuttered
or boarded up—
past the pool hall
with the door open,
the white shirts of the players
faintly luminous
in the dark interior,
the tips of their cigarettes
hesitating like fireflies
above the velvet table
while a Latin ballad
blared from a radio—
past the vacant lot
where a few smoky weeds
groped through the oily ground—
past the bodega
where a woman was splitting melons—
past the curb where despite the hour
a tiny girl sat beneath the wheels
of a parked car,

playing with a hairless doll—
I came across some leather-jacketed boys
who lounged under a streetlight,
smoking, and—unbelievably—
taking turns on a battered pogo stick.
Laughing, they called to one another in Spanish,
the glitter of crosses and saints
shivering around their necks,
the knives in their belts shining
as innocently as fish.

THE GHOST IN THE BASILICA

Leathery skin dry, like a snake's husk,
and so fragile we can see, even
in the half-light of Saint Peter's dome,
how it shines thinly, showing

sharp bones beneath. The glass
casket which encloses his form
is yellowed too; the edges of the panes,
set in their frame of silvered brass,

rainbowed like Vaseline: but the eye
of pilgrim or tourist is drawn inward,
to the folds of the gold-sewn ceremonial
robes, which sag with dust over

his mummified limbs. Rings huge with jewels
gleam on his fingers. Before the coffin,
a plaque in four languages tells us
this is the uncorrupted body of His Holiness

Pope so-and-so, who sat
on the throne of Peter centuries ago;
this flesh once supple, this blood
lit with the glory of Christ. What accident

of weather or humidity produced
a shriveled miracle? It hardly matters
any longer. An elderly nun, her own skin
pale and taut against her birdlike

cheeks—though living still—kneels
and crosses herself before the body,
the dark folds of her habit spilling
onto the marble floor. Columns,

twisted like rope, rise
to the dome's crown, a circle of light;
around the rim the muscular, frescoed
angels link hands, silently singing;

below them, we turn again to the great bronze doors
and the more reachable heaven of the streets—
the leaning, shuttered alleys above which
choirs of emptied shirts swell and dance.

WHY THE FRENCH SELDOM EAT CORN

When they heard the sirens again
they blew out the kerosene lamp
and came up from the cellar.
The house was still standing
but there was nothing to eat
except for some maize
airdropped by the Americans
several months before,
which they ground by hand
in the dark kitchen,
moistening it with table wine
because there was no water.

It made a bread like stone.
And the woman at the *pension*
told me the story
thirty years later,
as she sliced loaves
from the bakery,
cutting a cross into each
in memory of the dead.

THE WINDOWS

Earthquake, San Francisco, October 17, 1989

Overhead, great double-bladed
helicopters sweep the sky
with searchlights, the white
insignia on their sides shining.
The Big Dipper leans coldly
over the tops of darkened houses,
Mars, a pinprick of rusty light
at its tail. People are crowded
into doorways, radios propped
on the hoods of cars.

I meet some friends,
tired and shivering.
We share a quart of muscatel,
riding in an old Plymouth
through the Mission,
where rubble and fallen wires
still litter the nearly empty
streets, where the stained
glass windows of a church
are lit from within, perhaps
by candle light: eunuch
angels with bright wings
hovering over a blackness

blank save for the distant,
cruelly sharpened stars.

ATTENDING THE BISHOP'S MASS
Paterson Catholic Regional High School, 1982

Dwarfed by the darkened scoreboard,
the bishop raises a chalice.

I get awkwardly
to my feet
among the lay teachers,
feeling acutely now
how the moon
of the communion wafer
has never risen
on my tongue.

It's a scene torn
from a book of dreams,
or some past life
long since forgotten:

The scrubbed brown faces of children
singing in dusty gymnasium light.

Old nuns rising
to cross themselves.

The Christ of the painted banner,
beckoning with wounded hands.

LOSS
For Meg

The year I lost you
water ran in the pipes all night

and I dreamed of rivers
in a tenement near a railroad track.
Sometimes I would wake
to the long whistle
of some bedraggled freight
groaning past in the rain,
and sometimes to the coughing
of the old man one floor below.
It's funny, almost,
to think of it now—
I say, *I lost you*,
as though you were dead.
The truth is nothing
so melodramatic,
but subtler, like wind
sighing through bare trees;
and more insistent,
like a phone that goes on ringing,
or light from a star
blind for centuries,
still throbbing
in the winter sky.

HISTORY RISES

History rises unbidden in the schoolyards,
in old rhymes, whispers of the plague years
echoing across cracked asphalt,
mingled with childish laughter:

Ring around the rosy, the boils swelling
on the skins of ancestors who wrestled
with death on beds of dirty straw,
burning the slow fuse of fever

as the blood went bad. *Ashes, ashes*
is a ghostly sneeze down seven hundred years—
or else, the ash the dead bones blackened into
in some forgotten potter's field. And the quaint

pocketful of posy, so charmingly poetic now
in its innocence? An herbal cure,
helpless even then
against the reaper's shadow darkening

a cradle song. There are some griefs
so large they graft themselves
onto the language, lingering long after
both mourned and mourner fall to dust.

IN MEMORY OF WELDON KEES

"For those whose voices cry from ruins..."
    —W.K.

You had spoken of suicide
or of starting over somewhere,
Juarez perhaps, or the Sahara,
following on the heels
of the mad alchemist Rimbaud.
The poems you left behind
were like the daughters you never had:
hapless brides of an idiot world
crippled by syphilis and suspicion,
through which you used to wander
with a glass of dirty whiskey
fluttering in a hand jaundiced
by nicotine.
When they found your car
abandoned on the approach
to the Golden Gate Bridge
that day in 1955,

it stank of the sticky heat of summer
and the emptiness of the heart.
Your poems are not read often now;
I met them in a battered paperback
which cost a quarter,
buried at the bottom of a cardboard box
in a shop on Bleecker Street,
among the broken phonographs
and water-stained lampshades.
You would have appreciated that.
In the cover photograph you stand
smoking a cigarette and staring into a river
which time has dulled to the color
of an unwashed bandage
where shards of declining sunlight cling
like clotted drops of blood.

EVEN SO

It was December,
and the sky
was shaggy and chill.
I wandered alone
across a stubbled field,
my body
bitter with cold,
the ragged trail
of my footprints
crisp as a longing
on the new snow.
In the clogged branches
somewhere above me,
a wood thrush—
left behind for some reason
I couldn't guess

after its fellows were gone—
decorated the air
with one liquid note.
And I knew
that the season
was not about magi or angels,
but the joy that abides
in the triumphant wail of birth:
we hurt, and are not healed;
even so, we sing.

WHAT THE EYE IS DRAWN TO

In a daguerreotype the Marin headlands
are the scorched yellow of smoke;
a dark schooner drifts lazily
in the waters off the Golden Gate,
sails furled; the heavy walls
of Fort Point dominate
a treeless shore. What the eye is drawn to

is absence: the burnt-orange girders of the bridge
still a generation away, nothing spanning
this air but a few tattered ribbons
of soiled fog. The familiar here
is frighteningly foreign; the wrinkled hills
mock us with their timelessness:
this is our home, yet another

place entirely. Everything is more—
and less—than what it seems to be,
caught in the shimmering web
of history. From the same period, we find
a half-constructed Eiffel Tower
tilting skyward over the drenched,

gabled roofs of Paris, boulevards

lined with trembling trees
down which the horsecabs clatter;
or, in New York, sedate brownstones
fronting a ditch where the ribbed ceiling
of the new subway rests like the skeleton
of a beached whale, each perfect arch
gleaming with possibility.

A new world heals over the old,
leaving its scars on dulled tin.

THE STARS
i.m. Joan Yarns, died 1987

That final night, the cancer
smoldered in your nerves
like foxfire,
a shadow on your lungs.
I imagine your face
like the wax death masks
one sometimes sees in museums,
the sheet's stark whiteness
inviolate as snow,
plastic tubes jammed
through your nostrils.

You'd been dead for weeks
when I finally heard.
Then I thought about the stars,
how there are winds in space
whistling down the centuries,
galaxies that leave a scar like smoke
on a photographic plate.

And all of it gone—everything gone—
long before the news reaches us.

THE SEASONS OF A YEAR

It's strange how
each season announces itself
as a quickening of the blood
weeks before the calendar
officially ushers it in:
snow, though odorless,
fills streets with its smell
when it is barely October,
and a sunlit field
in late March
may wear the look of summer
even when seen from afar.
Sometimes I think
this is what makes the world bearable—
that the greatest love we know
is something deep in the earth,
and each of us in daily exile
still smiles at the sight
of wild strawberries ripening
beneath a barbed-wire fence,
like tiny red lanterns
lighting the way home.

OMENS AND PORTENTS

Without warning, holes
appeared in the soft earth,
dozens of them,
steaming a little
at the edges.

Although all the mountains
were silent
the elders of the village
prophesied doom,
a sky plumed
with fire and brimstone.
It's said though I don't believe it
that that year
a young girl
gave birth
to a goat.
What is certain is this:
attendance at Mass became more frequent,
as did occurrences
of the Evil Eye.
These things continued
for a long time,
even after the holes
had closed up—
as suddenly and silently
as morning glories do at dusk.

THE DEATH THIS YEAR

The death this year
has been an ordinary death
of the kind that attracts no mourners.
I have grown slightly older
in a town with many boarded windows
and streets smelling of urine.
I write poems
because I can no longer remember
the touch of my hand
on a woman's breast.
One has to love something.

THE WEREWOLF'S GRAVE
For David Watters

The caretaker points to where
three hundred summers
have worn the fur of moss
from the base of this stone
in the darkest corner
of the churchyard,
where the ground has shrunk away
like gums from teeth.
It takes a moment to notice
what the chisel has left
where the carver must have known
it would not see the light
for centuries—
a wolf's head
crudely depicted
by a wedged blade,
the eyes with their slit pupils
so cold you can almost see their shine;
the muzzle twisted
into a snarl;
the ears pulled flat,
pointed and sharply lupine;
but the rounded forehead
unmistakably a man's.
The whole town knows the story.
He was an elder of the church,
burned at the stake
for keeping the witches' Sabbath.
It's said he cast a demon's shadow
in the moonlight,
and none at all
in daylight.
It's said
he does this still.

SULTAN SCHOOL FOR HANDICAPPED CHILDREN

There are those whose limbs twitch
like the limbs of the hanged,
whose eyes are vague
as the eyes of statues.

I can still see them playing
on the broken swing set
or sitting mute and bewildered
in the sandbox,
bathed in damp light.

I'm there too, of course,
on the crutches of childhood.
Wherever I am
I am still there.

CROSSES MADE OF FLOWERS

Hoboken, Easter, 1987

In this city of blind windows
where vagrants
drag shopping bags
down streets where forsythia
blazes its innocent gold
against the walls of empty buildings,
there's nothing to say about spring
which won't seem thin or false,
like a gin-soured kiss.
Old men retired from the coffee works
doze in the parks,
colorless heads nodding
in the striped shade,
their eyes enormous behind thick glasses.

The women who bob like sparrows
along the sidewalks,
wearing the black scarves
of Italian peasants,
file through the doors
of the parish church
as solemnly as statues.
They are promised miracles—
but the raised wine
tastes of vinegar and dust.
The priest kneels
before the Lord whose naked body
is a limp sail,
the breath of heaven
gone out of it.
Crosses made of flowers
shine in the hollow dark,
their petals edged with brown
as though on fire.

DINNER WITH LISA

The tablecloth spreads between us
like recent snow,
light from your drink
risen like the moon.
Although you are talking
this is a silent movie,
the spaces beyond your words
as still as deepest winter.
And I wonder—
how many travelers
must have perished here
on the long journey
into your eyes?

FALLING OUT OF LOVE AT THE COLUMBUS ZOO

How different the living zebra seems
from the poised and painted horse
we loved in children's stories,
that carnival animal never quite real
who grazed on the golden savannahs
at the edge of our earliest memories.
His coat is not, as we imagined,
as sleek as varnished wood:
neither a chocolate sundae
nor an elaborate parquet of monkeypod
and sun-dimmed bone.
Up close, it is a fine mat
of hair in which the light gets lost
on its way through the gray afternoon.
And we never imagined these other stripes
that settle at such crazy angles
into the tired contours of his back:
they are the shadows of the fence
which holds him in
or maybe keeps us out:
even from here they have the cold
uncompromising heaviness of iron.
Look, you nearly whisper, how these eyes
always so merry in storybooks
are in reality only damp
pools of featureless black,
how they mean nothing
apart from what we bring to them.
How trite it would sound to tell you now
so much of ourselves is that way;
but my fingers slip like snakes through yours,
and your familiar feminine smell
is drowned in the pungency

of brittle grass and dung;
reflected in the zebra's eyes,
how small we seem, and separate—
like bubbles on a stagnant pond,
barely here, then gone.

SAINT JEROME AND THE SKULL

His beard nods in time
to the scrape of his quill.
When his dim eyes rise
they find the skull:
the dark omegas of the sockets,
an alphabet of gumless teeth.
The cracks that cross
its brittle surface
resemble rivers,
outlines of continents.
Already he guesses
the world is round,
hollowed out of the void
like a drowned man's breath.
The cave encircles him,
moon in its mouth.
He grinds ink from mulberries,
burns pale candles
smelling of lard and honey.
Slowly, the wide pages fill.

WAITING FOR THE THAW

For Mekeel McBride

When it comes we'll find
what the snow keeps hidden.

The skate key lost
before the war.
A crow who recites
the books of the Bible.
The organ grinder
and his rusty music.
A man selling poppies
two for a penny.

There will be caramel apples,
figs, bright oranges
like those in children's stories.
For now, we have only snow,
an old shoe to boil it in.
Nights, we shiver by the stove,
whisper of meadows
vivid with clover.
Steam blinds the mirrors.

Huddled in empty rooms
we hear the deathwatch sing.
We hope for a change of weather.
Drifts reach the windows,
inch under the door.
Our wives thread hair through their needles,
quietly sew quilts
spotted with lilacs, cowslip, jonquils.

FAMILY CHRONICLE

My grandfather Walter Maple
was the dentist in Grafton, Ohio
during the Depression.
Farmers who had no money
paid for pulled teeth with eggs or rhubarb.

Gold crowns he made by hand,
even years later, when I was little.
His white head bobbed in the faltering light
of a fire he kept in a woodshed
as he hammered strands of ruddy metal
into tiny, uneven moons. Already
his hands were shaking, blue
under the nails. Saturdays
rows of bullets like buds on a stem
hissed in a bucket
while he melted lead.
In the backyard a tart smell of gun smoke
mingled with lilac and apple blossom.
He shot at cans or paper targets,
too close to death to feel like hunting.
Sometimes at night I see him:
black shop dust
clings to his sweating face and arms.
As always, he is melting metals,
murmuring something, over and over.
It's so confusing, he says,
and the wind at the window agrees.
He can't remember anymore
which one's to kill
and which to heal.

WALKING BESIDE THE HUDSON

The gunmetal spire
of the Chrysler Building
rises through a glare so fierce
that it seems impossibly close—
as when the camera zeroes in
and the entire audience

instinctively blinks—
not like a scene
where I myself am present,
although I pass unobserved
on the opposite bank,
down a road worn white with use,
through rust-gnawed debris
and high grass.
More and more I am reminded
of the figure in the corner
of some Van Dyck or Breughel:
that plowman or woodchopper who,
humble and infinitely human,
follows behind
the immaculately groomed duke
with the wide plumed hat,
leading a mare draped in gold;
and who, although he isn't really
the central subject of the portrait,
has, one suspects,
more deeply touched the artist
than has his master.
Similarly, I imagine,
I am spending my days in a corner,
with my fairly ordinary sorrows
and my equally unremarkable joys:
an anonymous figure walking alone
beside a muddy river,
watching the water fill with light—
always aware of the missiles somewhere
poised in their gleaming silos,
ready to crack the earth like an egg;
certain that in my own life
love is still unimaginably distant;
and somehow blessed despite it all,
a smile surprising my lips

as a dark vee of geese,
stitching the air with their cries,
crosses the mirrored immensity
of the World Trade Center.

—Hoboken, 1985

THE BO TREE

For John and Madhavi Young

Not in some distant India
but in a suburban dining room
we find it, the faint half-shadow
of branches brushing lightly

over a weathered wooden Buddha
which stands in one corner,
hands pressed perpetually in prayer;

the frail curvature of the trunk
supported by a balsa pole;
whatever roots it has
hidden in a big wicker pot.

Inevitably this tree evokes
Gautama's journey to enlightenment,
but it seems more honest to say

that each bright leaf
is its own language, softly
repeating something I recognize
yet cannot quite make out

as I sit here
on afternoons swollen with summer,
watching light pass through the leaves
which pivot gently on their delicate stems—

the Bo tree shines
as though its very presence
on this weary earth
were a kind of blessing.

SOME KIND OF PERMANENCE

Where did I read
that the dead smell faintly of almonds,
that a footprint on the moon
will stay for eons, undisturbed?

Now that we come to it,
where did I get this idea
that love was supposed
to last forever?
Even in my earliest photographs
my face stares back at me
with the eyes of someone
whose life is already behind him.

Yet it must be our faith
in some kind of permanence
which makes us cling so stubbornly
to the coffee cup
a lover used,
which makes us cut out, every year,
newspaper clippings assuring us
that the swallows have returned
to Capistrano.

And in November at least there is the wet gold
of fallen leaves on the street,
the way when I wake and look down at the pavement

it seems for a moment like a dark river
stilled beneath my window,
and the people walking their dogs
seem to be walking on water—
as though, even in this life,
such a miracle were still possible.

THE WHITE PEACOCK'S THROAT

The iridescent blue-green
throat of the peacock, bluer
than turquoise, purer than the flame
which sleeps in the shattered
heart of the sapphire: this
is only an illusion, a trick of light,
a reminder that, like all birds,
he is a child of the sky, and cousin

to the hardened, azure skins
of snakes. Nothing is blue
here but what the eye chooses
to make blue; like so much
in life, the peacock's throat
is a matter of belief.
Likewise the fan of brilliant,
staring eyes the suitor spreads

when courting, though truly colors,
are the blind eyes of evolutionary
accident, sadly bereft of
the piercing, all-seeing stare
which gypsies and fortune
tellers have sometimes
attributed to them. But what

of the alabaster whiteness

of one bird who mopes alone
in a corner of the pen—
whether peacock or peahen
we can't tell—the nearly
albino outcast displaying
a translucent tail blank
save for the feather tips
sharp with sun? The white

peacock is shunned
by gaudy cocks and dove-gray
hens alike. A friend says he pities it
at mating time. And I think,
the bleached curve of this passion
alone of all the flock
is free of artifice;

this pale, searching throat
offers only what is there.
With people also,
a love too honest
is often lonely.

From
Hesitant Light
(1992)

SUNDAY MORNING, EARLY: THE RICHMOND, SAN FRANCISCO

On Geary Boulevard, light peels
off the onion dome of the Orthodox Church.
Buses dulled by dust descend
towards the stark needle
of the Transamerica Pyramid.
The choirs of my mind
are empty, nerve ends raw
with the white noise of hangover.

There is no great tenderness
among the darkened tattoo parlors,
Chinese restaurants. The tight
sky isn't large enough to contain
any God. Love drifts like flotsam
through the ruined faces
of old Russian women
on their way to Mass.

A PALMISTRY

When I study the hollow of my hand
closely, it amazes me to feel
lost there, a wanderer
in the pale country of my skin.
No, I don't believe the future
is sewn into these furrows,
a strange crop ready to sprout—
but if I look at my palm long enough
there comes a moment when I no longer recognize it,
like a blank page, a word repeated obsessively
until it loses all meaning. Then
it is ready to begin.

It can warm a cold knife blade,
or tenderly travel the body of a woman.

AN AFTERNOON BY THE CAROUSEL

For Deena Larsen

Unicorns and ribboned stallions
rise and fall silently on their poles,
their paint so thick it gleams like glass.
The sky's the color of a bruise, the sun lowers
uncertain ropes of light through the trees.
The animals' backs are nearly empty
except for a few old people, colorless and small,
who clutch the reins with unsteady hands.

Beneath the eucalyptus we stand watching,
our fingers linked although we are not lovers.
Tinny music settles over us like a bright pollen.
Your eyes, enormous through thick glasses,
memorize everything: the frail riders,
the horses' heads thrown back, their silent neighing,
the endless swirl of sun and shadow.
In the hesitant light your white cane
shines unbearably, a candle, a bleached bone.

SELF PORTRAIT AT 34: ON THE GOLDEN GATE BRIDGE

Beneath me the sails
of hundreds of boats
beat like wings against
the Sunday sky, the cries
of the boaters carried off
by wind, a festival in which
I do not share. Traffic fumes

burn my nose and throat
like the insistence of loss.

My life half gone,
I have accomplished nothing,
have nothing I can truly call my own.
Nor have I loved in any way that mattered.

The air around me is faded and brittle,
the moment vanishing even as I live it.
The shadows of towers bend on the broken water,
drawn together by the weight of the bridge between them.
Even the afternoon light seems heavy,
peeling in strips from the soft tar
of the roadway.

SPRING: TWO VIEWS

I.

These shadows are the hollow
longing bodies of the poor.
The eyes of one old drunk,
emptying, remind me suddenly
of the eyes of a dying fox my father
picked up on the roadside years ago,
clouded, utterly blank. I press
a coin into his soot-scarred palm:
he looks away. Above us,
in the narrow throats of sparrows,
the blind, obedient pulse of life
shrills a song older than language
into an afternoon pale and clear
as stretched skin.

2.

When they scraped the fetus away she felt nothing.
Now something has broken loose from her heart,
drifting like a fine ash, invisible,
over sullen streets where strangers
sleep off drunkenness in doorways,
light floods the pavement like water.

And it's spring. In window boxes
violets press through the ruined earth,
blue as clotted blood.

AT THE FUNDAMENTALIST CHURCH

It is not the way we sit together
high in the varnished balcony,
my arm around your shoulders
and you so close I can smell
the dark sweetness of your body heat—
nor is it the faint amazement
with which I watch those newly called to Christ
clad in smocks and holding their noses
as attendants immerse them
in a child's rubber wading pool—
it is not even the awkwardness I feel
at being so close to someone else's God—
it is none of this yet all of this which chokes me
as I rise clumsily with every hymn,
feeling a pure love, thin as light,
taking the voices around us
to places I will never go.

IN MEMORY OF
A FAILED MESSIAH

You once showed me the Book
you'd gone alone into the desert to write,
a suitcase full of jumbled typescripts
and jottings. In the next room your wife
lay gasping for breath on a stale bed,
cancer heavy in her lungs.

Long after everything was over
they found your car abandoned
on a bridge, note on the seat,
your body curiously intact
on the rocks below, something
like surprise on your face.
I imagine the highway patrolmen
and coroner gathered around you,
speechless, the sky above them
a dense water, a few faint stars
dropped through it like stones.

JESUS

1. Oil On Boards, c. 1480

His wrists are nailed to the wood,
blood clotting on the sharpened iron.
Carefully applied layers of pigment
lend the drops of sweat on His brow
the accuracy of a photograph.
We feel His thorned head limp and heavy as a stone.
This much the masters understood—
in the greatest art the intricacies of light
go hand in hand with those of pain.

2. On The Platform, 1987

At first I don't notice the heavy glasses
opaque as the night descending,
or how his alert, bitter eyes
struggle to discern the shape of an incoming train.
But the blind and the nearly blind
sense movement even in stillness.
In a tone like the hush of shared secrets
he tells how his vision failed after the war,
rotted by poisons he carries inside,
too deep to feel or ever wash clean.
He must be nearly fifty, gray at the temples,
loosened skin around his eyes,
but his translucent face has the clarity
of the work of a Renaissance master.

PICTURES OF THE DEAD

When she was young, my grandmother told me,
photographers clamped their subject's head
in a brace, to hold the face impossibly still

for the long minutes it took to burn it
into eternity. Perhaps that's why my ancestors,
with their starched collars and perfect mustaches,

all look so stern, so vaguely uncomfortable,
their eyes glazed white like the eyes of statues;
their memory reduced to a urine-colored stain

on a bit of tin. In France, I remember,
I visited a cemetery where photos of the dead
decorated every tombstone, encased in thin

frames of soiled glass. Sunlight and rain

and the years had faded them
to near invisibility, like

the aching that burns at the back of the eye
when one has looked too long
at a brilliant light.

NEW YEAR'S DAY: THE SUTRO BATHS

Abandoned decades ago,
the marble baths are naked to the sky,
brilliant with yellow-green algae.
Near one, a young couple poses for a photograph
with their arms tightly around each other,
the ragged expanse of the ocean behind them.
I'm too far away to hear their laughter.
The woman's hair spreads in the wind,
filaments of frozen light.

The year begins on a day without sun.
Hundreds of gulls crowd the tumbled stones,
doing their venereal strut
across the fire scars.

—San Francisco, January 1, 1988

SAN FRANCISCO, MY THIRTY-FOURTH YEAR

It is the hour
of the sleepwalker.
A plaster saint
glows in the window
of a storefront church.

An Eritrean nun boards a bus on Mission Street,
her heavy shoes catching on the high rubber step.
Somewhere someone is playing a harmonica.
Things stand out sharply, the way I imagine
they might to someone who is dying—
cold wind, an early moon,
sky still as a photograph.

I am nearly halfway through my life.
All day long, for no reason,
I have felt like weeping.

DREAMING OF AFTERSHOCKS
After the Bay Area earthquake of October 17, 1989

Again last night the ground was blackened
with cracks like the lines on my palms,
every fissure spelling fate.

If my hands were suddenly glass,
veins like wires bright with drumming blood,
this moment could hardly feel more fragile:
the rotted light, the park a bare field,
concrete benches like pauses in speech,
dark clouds of startled sparrows
shaken from the trees.

THE BODIES OF BONNIE AND CLYDE

In the ashen world before color
they lie together on a long stone slab,
surrounded by the curious—
her necklace dangling,
his thin tie drenched and dark.

This is what happens
when a legend is made flesh again,
slammed into sinew and gristle
by a hail of bullets.

Later will come the awful glory of it all.
The camera preserves them like this:
eyes opened wide, and empty,
a black spittle on their lips.

ILLINOIS WEDDING

For Laura and Jim

The dense air rises slowly,
folds of fine gauze carrying
upward the smells of varnish
and old sweat. Something's
burning just on the edge
of sight—or is it only
lack of sleep that makes
me think so? *What God*

has joined together
let nothing put asunder.
Not the stained sunlight
bleeding through the preacher's
book, not the notes stumbling
like ungainly birds
from the organ, not the hot fields
glimpsed through the window,
already brittle with autumn.

THE WEDDING PHOTOGRAPHS OF STRANGERS

The veils of these brides
are the color of dust falling through

weak winter sunlight. They must all be
old women by now, many long dead
or bitterly divorced, forever frozen here
in the flush of youthful optimism—
the brutish, drunken husbands,
feverish children, tenement hallways
smelling of cabbage, ahead of them still—
the years of war and famine, the loneliness
of ornate metal ceilings. How lovely
they are, every one! Their hair,
long and always dark, is luxuriously piled
into the elaborate *coiffes* of the end
of the nineteenth century. But their burnt tin eyes,
relics of the age of Daguerre,
shine when we hold them to the light—
like the eyes of frightened animals
caught in a headlight beam
just before impact.

THE APPIAN WAY, 1974

The roadside tombs have long been vacant,
featureless boxes of broken marble
from which the centuries have scoured
even the smell of death. In the distance
some crows squawk and squabble over something,
shaking the light like water from dark wings.

There are places where language fails completely.
What grammar could contain this emptiness?
The cypresses tremble with a wind too faint to feel.

MY FATHER EMERGES FROM THE DEPTHS

My father's aquarium
held tiny, clear fish that darted
like specks of glass through the green
water, their hearts and organs
bright threads of blood. I thought about
those glassy fish often during
the months he lived beneath the waves,

in a distant country, imagining
that as he breathed and worked in the steel tank
which kept him apart from us, his hands
grew clear and glassy, bones
shining through them, and tangled
blue ropes of veins. In dreams his eyes,
lidless and dilated, seemed to watch me
from an immense distance; his skin

had taken on the greenish cast
of the sea which covered him. At the base camp
his face on the TV monitor was a cheerful
mosaic of grainy gray light, his voice
familiar and reassuring even through
a maze of static; nothing was as I'd
feared. But when he and the others
finally emerged, into a rocking rubber

raft, we barely knew them at first:
there was a strange light in their eyes,
deep as the sea, and as hard to hold.

Robert Lavett Smith

OUR HIGH SCHOOL CHOIR PERFORMS AT A BLACK CHURCH

Union City, New Jersey, 1975

The choir robes are stiff,
awkward as wings. I'm uncomfortable
with the Vivaldi, wrapping my mouth
around notes that just won't come.
Then silence—as dark hands
raise the Host in the fractured
light of the rose window—a stillness
flaring out around the flickering
blood of Christ. At the reception
the congregation keep to themselves,
shy with these white kids from the suburbs.
Across the cake, girls with eyes as black
as their faces study us cautiously,
licking their lips, nervously crossing
and uncrossing their legs.

PATERSON

i.m. Joe Butash, 1909--1986

It's like a photograph I can't see clearly now.
In this or another, earlier life,
I rented a room from an elderly widower
in a house across from the cemetery,
rows of tombs glowing faintly
under a moonless sky the color of a scar.

There was a bed, and a small desk
with a crucifix adrift on the wall above it.
I remember trash blowing through the streets,
a darkened storefront church with its neon cross
printing the apocalypse against torn clouds.
The old man barely nodded as I climbed the stairs.

He sat alone in the darkness, invisible
save for a few white wisps of hair,
the clicking of his rosary huge in the stillness.

TWILIGHT, *CRÈME CARAMEL*, AND A WOMAN NAMED SHAWN

Let me not confess
to the long years rusted with loneliness
here at this table where the custard on our plates
gleams wetly in the failing light.
Your almond eyes, your smile
lie on my life like blessings.
In the plaza below us, strangers
stroll by the fountain,
the trembling water suddenly luminous.
There is a music in the heart which rises
even in silence, all the world
dumbstruck in its mute crescendo.

I DIE

I have dreamt my own body
laid out on the shine of funeral silk,
hardly older than I am now:
eyes sewn shut, features
empty as new snow.

Unnoticed, I move among
the mourners kneeling at the varnished coffin,
candle flames wet on the black of their clothing—
their eyes are red with weeping, while my own
are clear as stars at the last moment
before they dim into the sunrise.

None of this matters.
Already the velvet blossoms
on the wallpaper are fading.
I walk down a road at dusk,
under ancient trees—
a paper sky, no wind,
nothing around me breathing.

THE ROOMS WE LIVE IN

It is hardest to be honest
about pain. Pain is
the healed scar still felt,
the wound visible only by moonlight,
the distant view of the firestorm
when the mist quivering on the horizon
may after all be only rain.
We spend our lives denying
that we are suffering, exactly.
And the rooms we live in
are like tombs: table,
chairs, reading lamp
blurred with the dust
of all we might have been.

A BASKET OF SILK FLOWERS

For Mark Bitzer

Poor imitations really, the shapeless
blue blossoms of the zinnias whose petals
are faded to lead at the edges,
the pale lilies whose ridged wings
show too clearly the delicate
weave of the silk. Carnations
whose red has dulled

to the brown of dust, papery
as the ones schoolchildren used to buy
on Veterans Day, keepsakes of wars
they neither remembered nor understood.
A cloud of Queen Anne's lace,
white once perhaps, which clings
to everything like smoke. These flowers,

not subject to the sway of seasons,
seem haloed in their own slow decay,
more real somehow for their failings
than what they sought to imitate.
Like the tenderness in the arthritic
caresses of elderly lovers, they seem

strangely validated by all the things
they can never aspire to.

THE DEATH OF WILLIE DIXON: AS REPORTED ON NATIONAL PUBLIC RADIO, JANUARY 29, 1992

The deejay's voice, flat and atonal,
seems more suited to a Haydn symphony.
Instead he says, We've just heard
Mr. Buddy Guy, friend and colleague
of the late Willie Dixon, performing
a Dixon composition, *I'm...Your...
Hoochie...Coochie...Man.*

Later, they reach Buddy, touring
in the Delta, by phone:

Was Willie prolific?

Huh?

Did he write a lot of songs?

Oh yeah, he done *that*.

AT A CIVIL WAR REENACTMENT

The sulfurous stink of gunpowder
is real. The sun flares
on real muskets. Uniforms,
says a man squinting at the sun
through wire-rimmed glasses, are
as close to authentic as they can
make them, dyed the old way,
in vats of crushed acorns or flowers.
Flags of both sides
uncurl through the smoke that stays
close to the ground, spreading
over limbs perfectly stilled
in the awkward postures of death.
Screams drift from the hospital tent,
where women in hoop skirts
wield saws whose blackened blades
are honed past illusion. But
these dead will rise before
the trumpet sounds, brushing off
the film of dust which lends
their pallid faces a ghostliness
beyond even the most skillful
imitation. What is it
in the past that refuses to heal,
condemning us to replay the scene
exact to the placement of cannon,
the spots where bodies fell?
The grass is a low green fire,
rooted in real blood.

THE BRIDGE, SOON AFTERWARDS

> *"Let there be no hereafter;*
> *the contract is broken."*
> —Alison Lett, 1959--1991

From this height your body
must have shattered on the water.

The lies we use to comfort the living seem empty now:
I don't believe you're in a better place,
or even finally at rest—
though over the phone a friend said
she admired your courage.

Off the salt-gnawed rail to seaward
the ocean is a sheet of unbroken light.
But I'm told you jumped facing the city,
your last dizzying view a jagged skyline
throbbing beneath a vacant sky.

THE BLUE ANGELS PASS OVERHEAD

For Anna Balint

It is as if the sky were indeed
a high, fine fabric such as the alchemists
might have imagined, suddenly torn
asunder with a fury the medieval
mind could only have understood as
apocalypse. Even so mild
an afternoon as this reverberates
with something ominous, and hard
to name: as though
silence closes quickly over
a wound we feel but cannot

seem to find. We know, of course,

that somewhere far above us, where the world
is a bent rim of dazzling light
pressed against darkness, steel birds,
more grandly horrible than Dante would have dreamed,
bear men without faces
through a Heaven now sadly devoid
of even the angriest Seraphim.

AT BEAN HOLLOW

Such fragments as we have
of the true moon are more prosaic:
bits of iron or calcium
in whose darkness a few flecks
of silicon sometimes shine
(we can only say) like stars.
Their composition unremarkable, they acquire
at best the luster born of distances.
But these formations,
earthbound, astonish us
by their utter strangeness—
whether a briny wind
or the restless advance
of the ocean has sculpted
so perfect a smoothness
is anyone's guess. Honeycombs
of ruddy, yielding sandstone
appear all along this
part of the coast, pocked
with concavities and round
holes like the eye sockets
of vanished giants. The mind
rebels against simple erosion,

rejecting so intricate
a consequence of chance.
Yet what god would leave
as signature such a multiplicity
of emptinesses, however beautiful?

From

THE NOB HILL MARINERS

(1994)

Terri: Full moon rising on the waters of my heart.

THE NOB HILL MARINERS

All brass and varnished wood, the cable car,
from which we hang uncertainly, like sailors
from rigging, glows in the wet light
like an apparition, its antiquated
benches and poles almost unbelievable
against the chrome and dark glass
of the business district. We can

barely feel the mist, not really rain,
which dims the streetlights rattling past
to the softness of seamarks, as though
decades dissolve around us, leaving
only the night and the always-near
smells of summer and sea. And at the crest

of each hill the world recedes
as it must have once for the mariners sure
that every horizon was the edge of the earth.
Then down we go, laughing although
our fingers tighten automatically
around the handled edges
of our seats. And no one ever falls,
nothing is unsure. Yet we feel the wind
in some forgotten rigging, the clatter
of wheels like the straining
of lost, tar-darkened ropes.

A LETTER TO MEG IN NEW YORK

What of this harvest of broken fingernails,
lost promises, days torn from the calendar
like stitches from a wound?

If I had your address, perhaps I would write you,

say, I am in San Francisco now, live only blocks
from the Golden Gate Bridge, have watched the fog
tremble over the ocean at night as the lights come on,
the water darkening just like in the movies.

There would be no need any more to mention the night
we cried so hard that neither of us could speak,
the smoke from your cigarette tangled in the ceiling fan
of a small café, or the rain that began just at dawn
when you left me on the corner by the pool hall,
disappearing down the littered street without looking back.

I could tell you instead that roses pale with frost
still swell with sunlight, that the taste of Chablis
lingers like the tuneless strumming
of your old guitar, or that the cable cars,
clattering over the hills like ghosts all night,
always carry, windswept and laughing,
her dark hair spreading against the brilliant sky,
someone who might have been you.

A NOCTURNE FOR FISHERMAN'S WHARF

On the rocks below the pier
the air is thick with the stink
of rotting fish; oil spreads
in faint concentric rainbows.

The night is damp and silent
as a sanctuary: moon
its rose window, aisles
of splintered light.

FROM THE 41ST FLOOR

In conference rooms, polished tables
hold the reflection of the sky.
Plate glass windows, solid walls
of immaculate quartz, open
on the scene below—as though,
like Icarus, we have broken free
of the world, above which
we now drift in sunlight,
admiring the cars scurrying like beetles
over the bridge, the water
burning like burnished silver.
And there's always some freighter passing
far beneath us, docile
as a cricket, cranes and pulleys
on the deck working
like insect legs. Yet I love most

those summer dawns when a smoke of fog
whitens the surface of the bay
as it does in old Japanese prints,
when the gray hills
hang loosely over the earth:
then I sense the mystery
quivering always beneath the visible,
the way the pale morning yellows slightly
at the edges, like old silk.

DANA'S PIPE

Briarwood bowl, naturally
ornamented by the scars
of vanished branches,
which spread like leaves
over the shiny wood—

she fills the pipe
carefully, respectful
of its elegance, after
tapping ashes that smell
of spices into the ashtray
next to the stick shift.

We are parked by a dock
where gray water wrinkles
and surges over rocks,
everything the monochrome
of the brooding sky.
Striking a cardboard
match she inhales
slowly, aware of the
amused and curious glances
of couples strolling
by the rail. The leaden
sea strains around us.
And the pale sunlight
of overcast washes her face,
her hair salted
with just the suggestion
of gray, the skin
around her eyes
looser than I remember.

She is beautiful still
in her faded flannel,
but doesn't know it.
What goes unsaid between us
reminds me we are older now
than when we met, sixteen
years and an ocean away.
Then the tapping of her
incongruous Ashton

in the silence, the way
ashes fall from the moment
wordlessly, while light
pours without stopping
into the ragged bay.

FOR THE BUILDER
OF GOLDEN GATE PARK

John McLaren, 1846--1943

The white wings
of circling gulls
flare in the sun,
carrying his vision
beyond the sand
blowing loosely through
the roots of a few dead trees,
the blond grass
rotten with salt.
He sees fields of tulips
brimming with light,
rows of eucalyptus
silvering a wind
that tastes of spices.
Avenues and pavilions
rise in the emptiness.

Long afterwards they will tell
of the year he wanted for his birthday
only the manure to feed his flowers;
or how, when he was nearly eighty,
he worked all night with his gardeners
to plant a forest of saplings
in the path of a proposed streetcar line.

Visitors will see him
even after his death:
a bent figure
among the rhododendrons.

The light will pour
through the blue pines
until they shine,
willows tremble,
hibiscus and roses
spill from garden walls.

And once each century
a single, perfect blossom
will whiten at the heart
of the century plant,
on its crown of rough,
broad leaves.

SNOW IN THE BERKELEY HILLS

Here where the somnolence of summer
settles like dry rot,
where the first pale days of autumn
seem frozen forever
on the watery rim of the world,
the edges of things are blurred,
without texture or clarity.

Once, soon after I moved west,
a thin sprinkling of snow
dusted the Berkeley Hills,
for a few hours only—
a shimmering whiteness
so faint it might have been ground fog,

or the sudden blossoming
of countless tiny flowers.

What wind out of my own past
comes bearing clouds of ice crystals,
high and fine, the first flakes
sparkling like memories, like the longing
for a colder, more passionate climate?

TERRI ARRANGES THE MANTELPIECE

"If I forget my happiness, let me be dust."
—Harvey Shapiro

The gentleness in her eyes becomes
fear sometimes, the pain
of her broken marriage,
the struggle to raise
two small children on her own.
How lovingly her dark hands
arrange an Oriental fan
above the fireplace,
next to a doll in African dress—
every gesture saying
one can make a home
in even the most wounded life—
while ragged light falls through the blinds,
dust motes swirling sharp as sparks
around her, the shattered
pieces of her world somehow falling
into place.

GOLDILOCKS

For Ashli Woodfolk

She's four,
coffee-colored,

tight, bronze curls tipped
with sunlight, gray, curious eyes.
Scoots herself up onto the couch next to me,
stripes of light and shadow
falling through the blinds,
clutches a brightly colored picture book,
announces she's gonna
read to me. We both know
she is not old enough to read.

Eager fingers turn the heavy pages.
It's Goldilocks, or at least
I think so: *She go in the house,*
nobody home. She be
eatin' the soup...

Honey, are you sure
that's what it says?
Patient shrug. *Uh-huh.*

THE IMPORTANCE OF SPACE

On the first landing the docent tells us
how the cast iron stairs were brought
by horse and cart from San Francisco,
a journey of four days.
The light itself dates from 1872.
Between the outer
and inner walls is a cushioning
column of air, a concept remarkable
for its time. What strengthens the tower
is absence, and even now it's so perfectly straight
you can drop a quarter
through a hole in the topmost landing
where the counterweight cables ran,

and it will find the exact center
of the entryway a hundred feet below.

—Pigeon Point Lighthouse, June, 1991

THE SLOW LORIS

Neither skunk nor monkey,
the slow loris watches us
all day from the darkened halls
of the nocturnal animal house,
where the lights are kept burning
throughout the night,
in a curious reversal of nature.
For a quarter of an hour
we watch the loris shift the position
of one striped paw on its branch—
like watching the jerky, freeze-frame action
of a hand-held stereoscope
from the eighteen-nineties.
Its perfectly black eyes,
featureless and all pupil,
study us with an air
of bored indifference,
barely tolerant of the hurried,
graceless motion which palsies
even our loitering,
our most tender caress.
The loris knows
things take their own time,
and there is no hurrying
either life or death:
the way the sharks gliding
silent as angels
through the false infinity
of their circular tank

know without being told
neither to quicken
nor slacken their pace,
always to trust the current,
and that ever to stop is to drown.

SAND DOLLARS

They are more like the imprint
of ancient flowers
than like money:
until one bends to examine them,
they seem like plain white stones
such as the tide licks clean
and casts off everywhere,
unblemished save for one faint star
which lies upon them like a scar.
The star's imprint straddles
the sand dollar's back
the way a man might straddle
a woman when making love;
perhaps they are the children
of some mythic marriage
between sea and sky.
Or perhaps they sprang as they are
from the sand which nursed them—
and whose color and texture they share—
the way philosophers once believed
flies emerged whole and living
from the inert stink of dung.
Like bones, they have about them
an air of emptiness,
that sense of vacancy common
to houses where someone has died.
Like love, they shatter

when handled roughly.
We shall never understand them.
No one can name the kingdom
where they are spent like gold.

THE BOTTLEBRUSH PLANT
For Terri

In a cavernous Victorian movie house we saw a film in which snow was falling on a city of gaslight and hansom cabs. There was a party where dancers circled over a varnished parquet floor, while reflected candle flames pawed at their feet. High above the music, a man watched the swirling snow while his wife wept for a lover who had died years before.

Outside the theater it was still summer, and California a century later. A stranger in a ragged coat asked us for change on a corner by a pawnshop with the grill pulled down for the night.

That was the year I came west from New York, and was lonely; the year you walked out on your crack-addict husband with two young children in tow. We sat together in the smoky shadows of a small café—the blackness of your face seeming to absorb the darkness of the room, your eyes moth-white—and sipped espresso from little earthenware cups which steamed in the silence between us, while out in the street rain began.

Later, near an abandoned church, you showed me a bush I'd never seen before: a quiet blaze of bristles the color of blood, vibrant against the leaves' wet green. The bottlebrush plant. It burns, you told me, touching my hand. It burns in spite of everything.

DRIVING PAST

Through the car window
the white blur of your house, vacant now,
is like a ghost on a photographic plate:
something uncertain, always out of focus.

We were never really lovers.
So why should I recall so clearly
the sun, through blinds,
ruling your face into streaks of darkness and light
as you busied yourself in the kitchen,
droplets of soapy water gleaming
on the dark skin of your arms?

A TRICYCLE ABANDONED ON THE SIDEWALK AFTER DARK

Surely some child
will return to claim it
come daylight. But for now,
caught in the uncertain flicker
of the street lamp, it shines
on the rain-slick concrete
with the light of the one like it
you must once have owned—
the melancholy shimmer
of lost things.

FOG ON OCEAN BEACH

The stucco of the nearest houses
bleeds like a burn through so much white:
fronds of a few palms, brittle with winter,
hang as though by levitation

in their ghostly tatters.

I find myself marveling again
at how the known world unmakes itself—
how fog is like a deep blizzard
or desperate love,
stealing for awhile
one's sense of where things are,
while time within it grinds to a halt.

The rattle of distant streetcars swells
until it resembles no sound
I have ever heard in my life;
circling gulls
descend from nothingness
on dark wings.

THE BRANDENBURG CONCERTI

For Ryan Guth

Thirty-two summers
peel from my life
like sunburn. Gnats,
a swarm as thin
and languid as smoke,
writhe among the blossoms
of the mimosa. The concrete
streets are empty,
the light hard and dry.

More and more,
I pass the hours
wandering aimlessly
past turreted houses
laden with gingerbread,
parks with painted benches,

palm trees and pines.
These days are numb
as bandages over a scar.

I play my few tapes
over and over until
the music slackens
and stretches
into nothingness:
Bach late at night,
Beethoven in a room
with the blinds drawn.

For weeks afterwards
I taste the gentle
pressure of my tongue
on a woman's neck,
the sweetness of her skin
magnified by absence.
Alone in a rundown bar
painted to resemble
the tropics,

I lick the salt
from margaritas
while Nancy Sinatra
scolds me from the jukebox—
paper palm fronds
curling off the walls,
a tired string
of Christmas lights
blinking their way through July
into the tedium of August.

BAD FRUIT

My legs are purple with scars,
blue, stitched places without hair
that sear my skin the way traces
of old fires sear the land.
Something is amiss; something
the years of doctors and steel braces
couldn't put right. And somewhere
under the dark dome of my skull
a blood spot ripens on my brain,
like a bruise on bad fruit. A souvenir

of the birth no one expected me to survive.
But I entered the world, breathless
and nearly dead; beginning,
despite the odds, this crooked dance
which has taken me through
more than three decades:
this waltz with my lurching shadow,
this drunken reel with what
some stupidly insist is joy.

RAIN OFFSHORE

On nights like this when the wind sings deep in our bones,
even children feel there is something ancient in us,
and old people who've lived all their lives inland
wake inexplicably from dreams rank with sea salt,
though this is neither an age nor a country for omens.

There's a feeling that accompanies such nights,
a melancholy that washes in like kelp on the tide.
It isn't sadness exactly—no, not exactly—
it's as though our souls were a dark water
over which a wall of rain trembles,
approaching fast.

SIMPLY BEING HERE

These days I trust in nothing. There's
a light which blows like dust through
these empty concrete streets, on mornings
when the low wool of cloud just barely
lets it through, which seems genuine;
it reduces the world to a near monochrome

where details stand out sharply, and
the traveler regains for a moment the sense
of a real place; there's the harshness
of salt which clings to this Pacific air
in any weather, a faintly bitter taste
the sea leaves in our mouths, invisible
though it is behind the endless

San Francisco hills. There is the trembling
pollinated fire of the bottlebrush tree,
which burns without consuming: an almost
biblical miracle feathering the dark grass
of city parks. I have no grand philosophy now,
no overriding belief in the healing power of love,

no sense of any destiny greater than simply
being here. This is sufficient.
At night I lie awake listening
to the barely audible hum of streetlights
and the watery rush of traffic beyond.
The sky in my window is too charred for stars.
I rock in the city's huge and drowsy breath.

From

JESUS IN BED BETWEEN US

(1994)

For George Van Ausdall

AMONG BELIEVERS

In Paris, a Persian prophet
smiled benignly from the wall
while my signature unwound
like a hangman's rope,
marking a conversion
that would leave scars
on my wrists, months
of nightmares.
I was twenty-two,
lonely, bewildered by sex,
stunned by a brilliance
I thought was God.

Tonight in Berkeley,
more than ten years later,
I squint through candlelight
at the scroll to which the Nichiren Shoshu
direct their chanting, strange words
passing too fast to follow
in my borrowed prayer book.

The voices around me seem faded,
thinned by immense distance.

Outside, lamplight
quivers on wet pavement;
it is raining now, lightly,
just as it was then; the evening
throbs with the promise of storms.

CHINATOWN IN FOG

In a seedier part of town,
at least the hookers

with tight leather skirts
would be out, the Cuban
pimps with their dark faces
haloed by cigarette smoke
in any weather.

There is nothing here but rain,
a rain as old as the world.
No sparks crackle from the power lines
as an ancient diesel bus coughs helplessly
up the drenched slope of California Street.
The fish markets are closed for the night;
ragged alleys soften to brushstrokes
on a silk of fog.

Time bleeds through this neighborhood
like the dim half-figures bleeding
through the varnish of old paintings—
long-vanished years reappear like bastard sons
painted out of the family portrait.

EARTHQUAKE WEATHER

Nowadays we notice the little things:
ceiling cracks, the shaken blue
of cornflowers uprooted but still blooming,
slivers of glass shining among their petals.

This weather comes slow and heavy,
skies dull and still as the eyes of a corpse.
Radar and charts cannot be trusted.
When the moon bleeds, we know.

There are no old stories to save us now,
no omens written on the burning water,

no winds rustling the leaves
of charm book or breviary.

What language we have is rusted by silence.
Our children sleep but do not dream.
New lovers kiss quickly by candlelight,
their eyes unstill.

LIGHT AND DARKNESS

Shadows on the sidewalk
are sharp and still.
The furious brightness of asphalt
ignites the wick of the eye.
Heat clings to the skin
like salt. On the corner,
oranges spill from open bins,
so brilliant it hurts to look.
How can any of this possibly last?

Suddenly I know I will one day die.
I can sense the earth inside me:
my heart a knot of fire,
lungs like beating wings.

Someone has cut initials
into the brown concrete,
and a date, 1940. Walking over them,
I feel again as I have in the dampness
of cathedrals when I trod on the slowly dimming
names of the dead without meaning to,
blundering in the dark.

MEATLOAF

i.m. Solomon Dean Lipton, 1918--1992

As I passed a vacant store
on Clement Street, its windows
covered with yellowing papers,
my eye was drawn to your name
on a long-out-of-date obituary.
Just the facts: newspaper man...
one of the few to defend Tokyo Rose...
facial nerves severed during surgery...
book on the malpractice suit...

Nothing about the writer's workshop you led
for thirty years, nothing conveying the ornery growl
with which you pronounced Bukowski a slob,
Jack London a lousy writer—in general.

Nothing evoking the infinite precision
with which your hands, calloused and old
but still rock steady, placed a cigarette
into the corner of your ruined mouth,
half your face frozen, a leering mask.

And in a diner once, late at night,
near the end of your life, while the others
lingered over burgers and soda, I remember
you wouldn't even look at the menu,
and ordered the meatloaf and coffee,
just as a veteran reporter would.

OCTOBER MOON, NEARLY FULL, THROUGH CLOUDS

Doubtless it's only sentimental
projection which makes us insist

on the sadness of the scene,
but the feeling persists nonetheless—
a flat gray disc with one edge shaven off
just such that it resembles
a woman's head bowed in sorrow.
Luminous filaments of cloud
wreath it like fine hair.

Physics, or the logic of science,
do nothing to ruin the illusion:
above us, the lunar mother weeps
in an autumnal pietà ungoverned
by laws of motion or force.
And it's *the world* she cradles in her arms.

PEBBLES FROM A NORTHERN FIELD

These are the eldest of stones.
A honeycomb of tiny polyps curls through them,
a memory of ancient reefs—
like the thumbprint of the Mesozoic,
or some inscrutable cuneiform.

Plague scars, sightless staring eyes:
the pattern resembles corpuscles
squashed on a microscope slide,
droplets of the stony blood
of something unnamable—
something that might one day awaken.

THREE NORTHERN CALIFORNIA LANDSCAPES

1. San Francisco

A night like this could be an illumination
from someone's dream book,
or a *très riches heures*
for the end of this century.
Along Columbus the sex shops
print their promises against the sky;
even lust seems charged
with a benign and holy fire,
storefronts magnificent as mosques.
A stray gull, mistaken for a pigeon at first,
forages along the curb—
its alabaster feathers quivering with gold
beneath the Chinese neon.

2. Petaluma

Like many small towns, it resembles
an old photograph clumsily tinted,
colors fading gradually to a uniform gray:
the empty band shell, the stern, silent trees,
storefronts peopled with wooden mannequins
as old as the century. A man could die here
and hardly know it, the streets are so still.
The cypresses around City Hall
are barely visible—spaces in the sky,
empty of the stars that bloom
above the iron lampposts.

3. Montara Beach

Beyond the shallows the water dims to black,
a prairie of coarse grass stirred by wind.
This is the country that stretches forever
into namelessness. How easy it must be

for the drowned to dance here, unnoticed—
flesh less than a memory, light powdering
through their limbs, their watery gala lit
by the pale, rising lamps of jellyfish.

JESUS IN BED BETWEEN US

For Ruth Ann Nelson

We've just seen a movie
in which angels walked real and alive
through the streets of a modern city.
Now we're sitting in your car,
late, the engine idling.
You're talking about Africa,
how there is work to be done there.
Light seems to gather around you:
the headlights a gentle fire,
your pearl necklace and earrings
flaring like stars.

The years of my life
tremble on the brink of love,
as though on the lip of a chalice
from which I cannot drink.
When you mention faith I imagine
Jesus in bed between us, blood from His wounds
spreading its wings like a dark moth
on the sheets.

THE MORNING MAIL

Every morning I wheel a cart
through the dim, dusty basement,
towards the sound of choirs praising the Lord.
In the mailroom his radio is always loud,

always tuned to a Christian station,
towering organ chords cracked with static—
ominous music fills corners
where stacks of packages climb crookedly
towards the ceiling, envelopes
protrude like mute white tongues
from slots in worn wooden shelving.

And he's silent, unbearably silent:
translucent skin pulled so tightly
over a skeletal face that I suppose
this is no mortal man who watches me
indifferently through sunken, watery eyes;
whose bony hand relinquishes his fistful of letters
so gravely I'd guess they must hold
the fate of us all.

THE SCRAPBOOK

*"Be true to your color, because beauty
comes in every shade."*
—Essence, *March, 1993*

Nights, in an apartment
above a laundromat, late,
after the throb of dryers
has gone silent, strangers
asleep in adjacent rooms,
I paste pictures clipped
from Black women's magazines
into an album, loving the glossy darkness
of their limbs, the loneliness
in those almond, African eyes.

Surely this white man in my mirror,
this self I barely recognize now,
is an accident of birth, unwelcome

in the true country of my heart.

Morning brings flirtations on crowded buses,
my own eyes above the edge of my book
focused on wide, sensuous lips;
the curve of ebony breasts imagined
beneath blouses; faint, knowing smiles.
Amid the dark tangle and press
of perfumed bodies
desire arrives, unsummoned:
thirty-odd years of longing sharpen
to a point, delicate and deadly as glass.

THE BLIND CLARINET PLAYER

For Kimberly Browning

His one eye is a moon
adrift in its own orbit.
The other lid hangs empty,
a rag of bloodless
skin. He moves
with the beat, hair
fine as light: nodding to
the unseen drummer, avoiding,
by long habit, the pumping
trombone. Swing, Blues, Jazz:
a music has its own geography—
he finds his way by sound,
his horn a black cane
tapping at thin air.

NICOLLET IN WISCONSIN, 1639

On the journey upstream he dreams of the splendor
of the Great Khan's empire, speaks less and less

with the guides, stares back at himself from the river,
hair fanned out like the halo of a biblical sage.
Intricate mandarin robes—the best Parisian imitations—
rock brightly in the palm of a pale canoe.
This land is his to tame, and he intends to dress for it.

At last he wades ashore near a clearing
clogged with chokecherry, the air sparkling with flies.
A thin smoke mounts from a circle of ragged wigwams.
He strides across the stubbled plain like Christ
across still water, silk trembling on his limbs like fire.
The Indians watch him. He drifts through
the startled darkness of their eyes.
                    —*1994 version of "The Dragon Robes"*

MY FATHER TAKES ME FISHING

The wooden dock had its own
geography under bare feet,
fissured, then worn smooth:
sunlight clung in the cracks,
a wet heat. We laid the catch
there, silvery and damp;
his knife slit the bodies
soundlessly. He showed me things
no child truly understands—
gonads a purple thread like spittle
on the blade, the lobed white bud
of the brain, gills blackened
with their last desperate blood.

On the pier beside him
my steel leg-braces burned,
my premature birth and inturned toes
the aberrations of a defective specimen.

Thirty years later
our infrequent meetings
are splayed between silences
as though between microscope slides.
I am flayed by the disapproving
knife of his eyes. Wordlessly,
he catalogs everything
I have failed to become.

I CELEBRATE FIVE YEARS IN SAN FRANCISCO: OCTOBER 6, 1992

Another passage noted without fanfare.

The long hills climb
into a sky thin as beaten gold,
burnt slightly at the edges:
a sky as deep as the ocean,
and just as starless.

Cable car tracks hum faintly in the twilight.

Standing at the foot of California Street,
I look westward, uphill,
to where the Fairmont stands in silhouette
on the skyline, its glass elevator
a gently falling drop of light.

I know this city now;
sometimes, if I inhale deeply,
I swear I can even taste it—
a bitterness that lingers on my tongue,
like ashes mixed with salt.

EAST OF MODESTO

The stink of fertilizer
drifts among palm trees.
In the bleached light
they resemble columns
long since fallen to ruin.
I stand alone beneath them,
dust in my thinning hair—
scanning the horizon,
the years remaining in my life.

Beyond the ditches, refineries
fester in the fields: rotten with heat,
like something abandoned after a kill.

BEYOND RADIO RANGE
For Renée

1.
On streets rotten with smoke
under a sky blunt as a knife
you look over your shoulder,
gunfire snapping across a pavement
starred with broken glass.

Awake until dawn, you wear your poverty
like a tightness in the throat.
We call each other late at night
on days when I can reach you
where you work the swing shift,
machinery drowning the soft
pulse of the radio's jazz.

2.
For so long, sadness has covered me
like the daily dust habit makes invisible,

dimming the edges of things so slightly
I've sometimes thought I imagined it.

You've arrived in my life unexpectedly:
suddenly the zodiac of longing pulls apart,
signs recombine in unfamiliar skies.
But Wednesday through Saturday
you drift out of reach,
mute as an astronaut
circling the dark side of the moon.

AN AFRICAN CARVING

The black wood,
when sun strikes it,
is ringed with deep brown;
here's a woman's head
no larger than a fist,
heavy in the hand.

Her eyes, slightly uneven,
stare at something we can't see
with an air of disdain or deep concentration:
her broad lips are pursed and resolute.

Whether she wears a headdress
or ornately plaited hair is uncertain;
long earrings pulling her lobes earthward
make it clear she was a woman of wealth.

But hers is a face that keeps secrets,
serene and silent as the stones.
Her beauty has the soft finality of dust.

A DECORATIVE MANTELPIECE FROM EARLY IN THE CENTURY

How improbable a bit of architecture
it seems, since there's no chimney,
since a blank wall seals
the spot where the fireplace
should be, as though the fire itself
were a scar long healed over.

I'm told the mantel once enshrined
a gas heater back in the twenties;
sometimes I like to imagine
the wiggle of heat
rising on cold mornings decades ago:
for all its innocence, there's an ominous accuracy
to the way it lends everything the shimmering
impermanence of a mirage.

BUXTEHUDE BY CANDLELIGHT

For Ruth Ann Nelson

Wires down somewhere,
pockets of darkness bloom
on the city's dazzle.
The evening's concert
goes forward as planned;
we squeeze ourselves
into a blackened pew;
hastily placed tapers
flicker around us,
a light like water
washing over stone.

Seated beside me, you're beautiful
by candlelight—all the more so

because you don't realize it;
we are, and are not, alone here;
the audience around us is invisible,
a softness of breath and body heat.

My faith is less sure than yours,
pinned in the shadow of the Cross—
then the singers' voices
ring through this blindness,
sudden and clear: each note
a tiny exploding star.

WEDDING: THE ANNUNCIATION GREEK ORTHODOX CHURCH, MODESTO

For Chris and Elaine Chyrklund

Behind the altar
the Holy Virgin
rises through beaten gold,
the infant in her arms
already the Savior—
a tiny, beardless dwarf,
one hand raised in blessing.

An elderly priest opens the Bible
with translucent hands, bright pages
stirring like wings beneath his touch.

The bride's gown aches with light;
her groom stands serene in tails,
still as a ghost in a tintype.
When the priest crosses
the crowns above their heads,
they tremble an uncertain moment,

glittering tiaras ignited
by the candelabra.

And a marriage begins,
with a silence deeper than prayer—
like the silence in great music,
when all the choir burns
with one held breath.

A HALF-EMPTY PACK OF CIGARETTES

I choose her from the lineup,
scarcely believing I'm here:
long-legged and slender, chocolate complexion,
eyes so liquid black the scant light
seems to fall into them endlessly.
In a room lit by a frilly red lampshade
money changes hands, the tight sequined dress
peels off easily beneath my trembling fingers.
I am thirty-five, lonely. It's my first time.

What happens next could almost be love,
her softly coaxing whisper in my ears,
radio low—*hold me closer, tiny dancer*—
spring rain kissing the distant interstate.
I will feel her nakedness against mine for days.
Afterwards, in the bathroom, I lean over the toilet,
my own cock strange and thrilling in my hands.
Light drips from the crumpled cellophane
of a half-empty pack of cigarettes on the tank—
left behind by someone else.

A VIETNAMESE GRASS BEVERAGE: THREE POEMS

i.m. Victor Buxbaum, 1961--2013

1.
The taste is pungent, like a smell:
a dark liquid through which rubbery seeds
drift like the eggs of something indecent.

2.
This drink goes deep, igniting memories—
somewhere far back in time, the sun-tipped
trembling hills were all our world;
the wind in the grass was God, was the first
caress of sex, the memory of a sea
more ancient still.

3.
It's easy to imagine the sort of place
where they might serve it: a rundown luncheonette
with grease-stained walls, a languidly
turning ceiling fan. The indifferent waiter
bearing a can covered with an inscrutable script,
who turns away quickly
as you take the first astonished sip.

CURIOS

From

STURGEON MOON

(2017)

"Ask me who I *was*."
—Marley's Ghost

THE WEDDING

i.m. Adrienne Stengel, 1958–2006

There's your bright breath,
A bride's veil, dispersing.

The tear-drop heart,
Luna's dark oyster.

The moon, a ring
Of pale blue stone

Cracking,
Borrowing light;

The plate where
The wedding guest

Watches his face
Grow old.

There are dry leaves and wires
Vaulting an aisle;

The asphalt,
Black velvet.

A bat's twittered blessing
Under a streetlight.

Lastly, the trees
Holding their peace,

The hushed futility
Of vows.

LULLABY AND DIRGE

Once a day it happens,
always on time:

The night comes down,
swift as a stone.

Under its weight,
your first shoes turn to bronze;

the bride's straw flowers
ignite, becoming stars;

your ancestors' bones
rock uneasily on their porches,

blank grins
full of gold.

Sometimes the darkness
moves in a wall across the fields,

like a storm front,
a tidal wave:

those it surprises
can only stand and wait—

open-mouthed,
frozen with hoe and shears:

a crow nodding
on either shoulder.

SCÈNE DE GENRE

A stark, white room,
bare except for a table.

A rough wooden table,
cracked and stained.

The round peasant bread
like a moon in its center.

A woman cutting a cross
into the loaf, for the dead.

The rood which blackens
under her furrowed skin

like the shadow of
some monstrous bird.

APPLE TREES
Cold Soil Road, Lawrenceville, New Jersey, 1984

Since this is February
their branches now
thin to a nothingness
through which wind whistles.

They nod like old women
in the cold sunlight,
casting hideous shadows
across the ditches.

How easy to imagine
they once were witches
surprised by the sun
at some pagan rite.

And now I seem to see
some zealous preacher
of the nineteenth century
striding among them.

Vainly he gesticulates,
the pages of the Bible
he cradles in his palm
flapping in the wind.

ANSWERING THE RIDDLE

The egg arrives first,
by bus.
Response to an anonymous
phone call.

The chicken is late,
has come on foot,
crossed many roads
to get here.

A grimy corner
by a Seven-Eleven,
darkness falling,
large raindrops.

Neither knows
why they have come,
what this will accomplish.

The chicken ruffles her feathers,
struts impatiently,
stamps out a smoldering butt.

The egg of course is silent,

translucent,
moon-like in the gloom.

Inside the shell,
a phone is ringing.

PRIMER

First page almost blank
for the years
you can't remember.
A spot in one corner:
ink, dust, a fly?

Next, names of flowers:
silver bell
trout lily
bachelor's button.
This page is meadow green.
A breeze lisps your name.

Women's names now.
Audrey, dark eyes.
Rain in Erica's hair.
Rachel gathers wild mint.
Ruth feeds sparrows.

The lists get harder.
Words like
derelict, exile.
Words it may take
lifetimes to learn.

Lastly, the words
an old man says in his sleep

on long nights
when winter thickens
at his window
and there is none to hear.

THE PEACEMAKERS

New York, June 12, 1982

Above the bristling crowd,
choppers dart like startled bees
between towers with a sun
in every window.

If the world must end,
let it end now—
with bagpipes, singing,
ribbons, bright balloons.

If the wind
blows flesh away,
our bones will lie down
on Second Avenue,
hand in hand.

When darkness fills
the emptied city,
they will keep shining.

AUDLEY END

i.m. Franz Wright, 1953–2015

In a fountain
you see your face:
skull white,
a tourist's penny

in each eye.

Who comes a visitor
to a palace
without dressing
for the dead?

They smile
from every wall.

Look how they welcome you
into silk chairs,
canopy beds
fringed with dust.

Here you can dream
the dead's dreams
which are like those
of the blind from birth.

HEARSES

Let us begin
with the tassels
for the undertaker's horse,
hung on a rack
in a dim garage.

The high wooden hearses
are here too,
shining like leather
in the gloom.

They're the kind
that still have
those brass candle holders.

The velvet curtains
are pulled aside
enough to allow
just a glimpse
into each dark interior,
into things to come.

Of course they're empty.
There's nobody here but me,
and I wandered in
by mistake.

NOCTURNE

I wake before dawn,
suddenly sure
that another
is also awake,
wandering now
down ruined avenues,
past houses
dark with sleep.

The moon leans
over his shoulder,
a dusty mirror
just out of reach.

Why do I feel
his presence
so strongly,
his immense loneliness?

When I go to the window
the street is empty.

It's bitterly cold.
Light slants
through blinds
into the room,
leaving long scars
on the walls.

—Hoboken, New Jersey, 1983

WATCHING A BLIND MAN IN A SUBWAY STATION

What appalls
is how the white cane
hovers a moment
in the vacant dark
above the tracks
still trembling with departure.

In dreams I sometimes become
the one I have so often seen,
my eyes the empty moons
hidden behind his black glasses.

Mine too are the first
hesitant steps
on the metal stairs,
among the throng whose faces
are turning to stone.

KNIFE GRINDER

Consider that figure
from childhood,
the old man arriving
just at dusk

in an ancient jeep,
ringing a bell.

How solemn
we must have seemed
as we gathered
the kitchen knives,
blades flashing
in the sunset.

We watched like worshipers
as he bent over the wheel,
blue sparks flying
into the dark.

He sang as he worked,
in a language no one knew.
His song seemed to be
the knife of longing
sharpened for us all.

THE UNFINISHED THRONE

> *Convinced that the Judgment was imminent, James Hampton began in 1950 to construct an elaborate throne room for Jesus in a rented garage in Washington, DC.*

He dreams of bright rolls of tinfoil,
the garage with its dirty light, the low,

bare ceiling beams. Endless patterns
in smeared chalk, shears clipping thin,

wrinkled metal into triangles, diamonds,
dove's wings. Hours of patient folding,

his quick fingers bent in a constant,

dancing prayer. The work whose details

he mouths like a litany. Daily, the dark
odor of glue intoxicates him: an incense.

Then he begins to die. There at the foot
of the unfinished throne, among glittering

piles of scepters and cardboard crowns.
His body used up, stunned by familiar glory.

And the folded cot in one corner spreads
to receive him like a pale, upturned palm.

THE FLOWER BURNING

In all the coastal villages
they are burning flowers.
Soldiers ease dark trucks
through narrow, twisting streets,
past shuttered houses with low tile roofs.
Flanked by motorcades,
convoys hurry along a mountain highway.
Below, the cliffs plunge
into a faded sea.

A barbed-wire fence
surrounds the abandoned scrapyard.
In the towers, guards
clutch machine guns.
It is here that the flower burning
will take place.

The scrap heaps are covered with bright petals,
still damp in the first
gray light. You hear the gruff

idling of engines
as headlights are switched off.
The heavy sweetness
of thousands of flowers
hangs over everything.

The ovens have been glowing
all night long.
Rows of men in greasy overalls
shovel roses and sweet rocket
into the flames.

When morning comes, bony children
throng around the fence,
ragged and barefoot.
Their wide eyes shine
and flicker.

Above them, great columns of smoke
knot into dark blossoms.

DANCE OF THE DRESSES

For Elizabeth Hornor Boquet

Nights are lonelier
since your father left.
Now, the divorce final,
you sometimes tiptoe
to your mother's room,
knowing she is lonely too.
She sleeps on her side:
Your girlish body
fits snug against hers,
your feet reach past her knees.
Waking a little, she
rubs a hand through your hair.

Tonight the closet door
quietly slides open:
her dresses, empty,
waltz through the room,
hollow skirts and blouses
filled exactly to her shape.
Mom, you whisper,
the dresses are dancing.
Nuh, she says, barely stirs.
But she sees them too.
Rehearsing old steps
from memory, open sleeves
embracing an absence.

IF I HAD MY DRUTHERS

The dead would
bury us.

They'd erect
in our memory
the stony life's-head,
its eyes swollen
like ripe apples.

Our bodies
would be leaves
drifting
on a dark river,
all their color
washed away.

The carousing dead
would dance above us
in the heavy,
tramping wind.

EVERYTHING MOVES WITH A DISFIGURED GRACE
(2006)

For Pat, with all my love:

> "Every heart
> To love will come,
> But like a refugee."
> —*Leonard Cohen (1934–2016)*

Patricia Lewis Smith, 1953–2005

Part One

DON'T LOOK NOW

THE SKULL OF BILLY THE KID

> *"Three months after the Kid's death, a Montana newspaper reported that his body had been dug up, his head removed, and the skull polished in a manner appropriate to a relic."*
> —*from an article in the* New Yorker

Outlaw or not, William Bonney was a devout
Presbyterian and a former Irish Catholic
whose death elicited the usual dreary hymns.
Candles surrounded his handsomeness
like gun barrels aimed towards heaven.

Shot in the desert, miles from anywhere
last rites could be said for his soul, his body
grayed with the dust which would reclaim him.
And after his death the halo of his youth
and exploits burned ever more brightly.

But this other story interests me, the skull,
stolen by nameless admirers, rubbed until
it shone like onyx. His wanderlust outliving him
as it toured the West in some snake-oil show,
nestled in cheap velvet, five cents to see.

Why disturb its dark sleep? Murderer,
martyr, sinner or saint, Billy belongs to history now,
where the dead are restless, and never wholly themselves.

I can almost feel its weight in my hands,
the cracked surface cool and smooth, brown as a stone.
The pooled sockets which held his eyes regarding me
without apology, as if surprised to be here,
on the threshold of yet another century.

THE FINAL HOURS
OF THE TWENTIETH CENTURY

A few strands of cloud
dyed pink by the last
of the sunset, above
a street of tenements
where the lights
are just beginning
to come on.
And the sky,
a turgid water—
where the first stars appear
like flotsam after a shipwreck.
— *San Francisco, December 31, 2000*

FROM ONE WHO HAS
NO RIGHT TO GRIEVE

i.m. G. William Lewis, 1923--1998

Late afternoon. We sit by the window,
in the house you built with your own hands
when you were the man who held his smiling bride
in the photographs fading all around us.

Your eyes are heavy, nearly opaque.
The Bay is flat and bright as steel,
the hills above us luminous
against the threatening sky.

"Looks like rain," you manage to say
before sinking back into the sleep
which seldom releases you now,
struggling under its dark weight.

An order of service lies on the coffee table,

left behind by the deacons who came earlier
to give you communion, its white pages spread
on the dim wood like the promise of heaven.

But I'd rather pray for those
who must remain here without you.

When you are gone—soon—I'll have
no right to grieve, for I barely know you;
I'll marry your daughter at a wedding
we both know you won't attend.
I promise to love and treat her well.

And I promise always to remember you,
the way each gesture apologizes for who
you no longer are. "Strong," you insisted
when we first met, "I used to be strong."

MY GRANDFATHER'S VIGIL

i.m. Dr. Walter E. Maple, 1899–1969

In all my memories of him it's early evening,
dust-furred sunlight spilling through lace curtains
in the bay window. He's crumpled in the high
burgundy armchair, a gaunt, gasping silhouette.

The veins in his forehead are roots,
tiny and blue beneath translucent skin;
his hair by now is white, thinned
until nothing remains of it but light.

His head's thrown back, eyes closed, mouth open;
he struggles even in sleep to haul coarse ropes of air
into lungs already ruined by emphysema. Barely six,
I know instinctively he hasn't got much longer to live.

A rifle from the basement cabinet rests on his knees,
its oiled barrel gleaming as night falls. He's slept with it
for years, no explanations, won't be dissuaded. He rages
at any who dare suggest that this is, at best, foolishness.

My grandmother's hidden the cache of bullets he made
by hand at his forge in the shed, buried his gunpowder
with the beans and summer squash. Still, there are rumors
in the neighborhood, whispers in the pews on Sunday.

Of course I won't realize that for years. For now, somehow,
it doesn't seem strange to be playing here on the carpet at his feet,
admiring his gun, the bloodless knuckles of his hands, and in the
window behind him, the star-gnawed sky darkening above the elms.

THE CLOCKWORK FARM

Insert a quarter, and tiny carvings
spring to life. A yellowed sky
encloses it all; invisible gears
animate a scene excessively quaint,
unreal even to those who built it.

I remember the rough country of pain,
a wilderness of crutches, braces and canes.

The awkward dance of those days
is mirrored in these dusty miniatures,
bound by an awful gravity through which
everything moves with a disfigured grace.

LANDSCAPE WITH FIGURE, STANDING APART

Behind houses where streetlights
are just now beginning to flicker,
the lake deepens into twilight:
nearly invisible through pale trees,
its shadowy waters sharp with stars.

The first soft rustle of evening spreads,
becoming something not quite a stillness.

One by one, windows blink on
like dreamers roused from sleep;
silhouettes quiver behind bright curtains.
But the blind eye of the rising moon
reminds me I haven't come to stay.

Already they study one another shyly,
anticipating passions I won't share.
Only hours from now, on dozens of streets,
in hundreds of identical rooms, clothes will fall gently
from aging limbs, and from the astonished bodies
of those first discovering love.

I consider it all with a kind of nostalgia,
the way a patient recovering from amnesia
looks back with surprising tenderness
at the blizzard receding in his head.

Bearing the darkness before me
like a lantern, I move on.

DEAF WOMAN WRAPPING CHRISTMAS GIFTS AT BORDERS

She cannot hear
the tiny, elastic sound
of cellophane tape
being torn from the dispenser,
the minute crackle
of the wrapping paper
her quick fingers crease
and fold expertly over,
nor the infinitely small
kisses her fingertips make
against the tense drum
of the shrink wrap
enclosing a CD—
this thing which is, itself,
the palpable manifestation
of what she cannot miss,
having never known it;
what she cannot imagine
even as it enfolds her,
as present and unnoticed as the air.

DUST BOWL FUNERAL

For James Weddington

Near dawn, the farm hands dressed by candlelight,
their hair tonic thick, and rank with kerosene.
They fixed stiff collars to their starched white shirts,
and rinsed their mouths with urine to sweeten their breath.

They dressed in black, in suits they knew they'd wear
when, one day, they were laid in their own graves.
Such finery as they possessed was grayed
by the dust that covered everything like despair.

Dust storms had scoured the whitewash from the walls
of the clapboard church across the barren fields.
They walked together in silence, knowing the way;
in silence, after the service, they carried the coffin.

Six mourners bore that body through a landscape
as still and colorless as a photograph;
the only sound besides their own footsteps,
dust devils howling through abandoned farms.

The dry husks of dead locusts were impaled
on barbed wire fences: many thousands of them,
so that the wires sagged beneath the weight
like branches burdened with some hideous fruit.

GARDENING ALONG THE FIRE SCARS: OAKLAND, 1993

For Larry Conrad

Beneath the hissing of the hose
the compost pile smolders under fig trees.
"That's cooking nicely," you say, and I smile,
pleased with the metaphor. But you mean it,
grinning as you remove your heavy gloves,
determined to prove the thing's on fire.

And so it is, exactly as you claim.
When we reach into the mulch's hairy flanks,
it's hot inside, like reaching into a living thing:
a handful of dead leaves is moist and heavy,
as I imagine a beating heart might be
were one somehow to hold it.

Across the ridge, where the ground is barren,
they're rebuilding from the blaze two summers ago.

Rising through fireweed, skeleton houses
blacken against the conflagration of sunset.

As the first stars sharpen on the horizon,
we stand in the softly breathing yard, among
the darkening smells of mown grass and twilight,
wrapped in the world's slow, steady burning.

DON'T LOOK NOW

Somewhere above us,
gargoyles cough in their gutters.
Library lions yawn and lick their paws.
In formal gardens, sundials
lean discreetly towards the light,
pliant as heliotrope.
The mirror admires
its own reflection.
Scissors dream
of a whetstone's kiss,
opening and closing
gently in their sleep.
If you listen, you can hear
the asthmatic rasp of the wine.

IN THE NAME OF SCIENCE

i.m. Marjorie Ransom, who told me this story

This death is quietly awful in its immensity.
Near sunset, a mountain of gasping flesh
struggles into the shallows, then gives up.

It's a humpback who's strayed too close
to shore, stranded by the retreating tide.
Flanks bright as glass at first, then swollen,

cracking in the stale air, starting to stink
beneath a glittering cloud of flies.

Soon men from town arrive, furred beams
of headlights quivering along the surf line,
thinning to nothing before the ocean's
endless emptiness. They've brought ropes
and tackles, saws honed to pure cold light.

But who are these two tiny figures
astride the whale's barnacled back
shouting obscenities in pantomime,
gesturing wildly to the roaring night?

For years the locals will tell anyone who'll listen
about the time the biologists fought over a flayed humpback.
Laid bare by their tools, entirely indifferent to argument,
the disputed organs gleam wetly in the moonlight.
The liver bloated with the dampness of decay,
the stilled heart enshrined in its vault of ribs,
the lungs like sails becalmed in the briny darkness.

AFTER BRAIN SURGERY

Eight weeks in coma, endlessly adrift
Atop the blue inflated mattress meant
To stop your skin's erupting into sores.

Beneath the monitor's insistent scrawl
The dim moons of your eyes turn from the sun,
Blindly pursuing orbits of their own,
Shackled to sleep's interior gravity.

Your parted lips are working wordlessly
Around the swollen silence of your tongue.

The dumb obedient sprouting of your hair
From your shorn scalp amounts to nothing more
Than the body's reassertion of dull need.

If only I were sure your twitching eyes
Were more than random electricity,
I might not feel your absence quite so keenly—
The sheer brute force of it against my world.

CLASSICAL MUSICIANS IN THE SUBWAY

"Tant pis pour le bois qui se trouve violon."
—Arthur Rimbaud

There's a sadness in even the most jubilant music,
a hint of death. Consider, for instance, the rosined
horsehair in the violinist's bow, which slides so easily
across the lengths of tightened catgut, drawing out
that brief, exquisite cry of perfect pain
which we call *art* because to name it truly
would be to recognize the murder in it:
the violin, the cello once were trees,
green, growing things whose leaves
sang the subtler songs of the wind.
Yet the beauty of music is that it perishes,
each individual note a moment in time,
the melody discernible only as memory.
Not that that matters in this airless place
where multitudes rush blindly through the dark....

KICKBALLS

Even now, at the start of a new century,
they're identical to the ones we chased
across the asphalt schoolyards of the '60s

while our older brothers fell in Vietnam
and Kennedy, in flickering black and white,
promised Americans we'd reach the moon—
the moon, which was itself a yellow kickball
some kid's well-planted foot had sent sailing
over the backstop, beyond the cyclone fence.

BRIE AND CHIANTI AT MIDNIGHT

In a tiny hotel room in a city renowned
for its medieval bridges, we share quiet
caresses, brie and Chianti at midnight.

We have learned silence on our
journey together, passing through
lands where our words were useless.

My eager hands navigate your face
in the darkness: an oddly joyous act,
like reading a Bach sonata in Braille.

AT LAST, LIKE SLEEPERS

At last, like sleepers timidly emerging
from dreams of blindness, we awake to love,
finding our once-familiar lives transformed:
well-trodden paths lead to strange destinations,
and books we knew by heart delight anew
with passages we've never read before.

The light that fills our world is no longer
confined to wavelengths visible to the eye;
instead, it seems to rise from deep inside,
a radiance not so much observed, as *felt*.
No color on the palette quite describes it;
no words we know are equal to the task.

BOB DYLAN IS STOPPED BY HIS OWN SECURITY

> *"Even if they knew who Dylan was, the guards had strict orders that no one was to get backstage without an official credential."*
> —*from a newspaper report, November, 2001*

One can imagine the ice in his blue eyes
as they narrow to appraise these young upstarts
whose tattooed arms are folded across their chests
in a posture suggesting they will not be moved.

Beneath a wispy mustache, his lips curl
into a sneer resembling the one
with which a youthful version of himself
peered warily from the sleeve of his first album.

Four decades since have creased his weathered face,
hollowed his once-round cheeks until they seem
as ancient as the endless roads he's traveled:
now he looks older than his sixty years.

Yet—for so small a man—he carries himself
with an enormous dignity that suggests
the poise of Big Joe Williams or Lightnin' Hopkins,
earned from a life steeped in the Delta Blues.

He stares the shaven-headed giants down
without a word, his silence withering.
Unnerved, they step aside to let him pass,
trailing the weight of history in his wake.

THE TROUBLE WITH THE GARAGE SALE

Nothing has readied me
for such bottomless hunger.

Geriatric Russians,
frail and white,
arrive by the dozens:
so wraith-like and fragile
light seems to fall through them.

They're tougher than they look.
Gesturing madly with canes,
they spill from garage
to unguarded apartment:
a hydra of grasping hands,
gibbering as if possessed;
tearing down pictures, looting
closets, ripping out the phone.

(I know whatever nights
are left here will be gnawed
by dreams of appalling need;
moonrises swollen with leering,
translucent faces: aged grotesques,
finely veined masks of pure greed.)

And it goes on. A red-faced man
whose breath is rank with vodka
astonishes me by insisting he'll buy
my unpaid phone bill, mislaid on a table.

In minutes only hooks and bare walls remain.
These, and my cash box, still woefully empty.
Over my protests, hulking matrons load
dirty dishes from the sink into huge purses.

DREAMING IN BLACK AND WHITE

I live alone in a desolate neighborhood,
a world delineated in shades of dirty gray.

The mechanical whine of an ancient elevator
troubles my sleep; sweating through steam heat,
I leave my window open on even the coldest evenings.

It's like an old joke whose punch line's forgotten.
On the corner, Latino drag queens smoke,
idly swing purses, adjust padded bras.
Their eyes drift on the darkness of makeup;
veins swell horribly on their thin arms.

I observe life with the dispassionate eye
of a journalist's camera recording a massacre.
I sleep poorly, can barely imagine sex;
if I ever loved, I don't recall it now.

What spirituality endures here
emanates from a storefront church,
once a movie theater, half a block away:
the marquee proclaims all are welcome;
the letters are askew, unevenly lit from above,
where the assurance that *Jesus Saves* is tattooed
in flickering neon on a dense, immobile sky.

Nightly, in the littered street, sirens rush
towards disasters that don't concern me;
an old woman screams at no one in particular,
screams and screams in the endless drizzle.
—*San Francisco, Good Friday, 1995*

ETTA AND THE SEAGULLS

Etta James, performing within sight
of the Golden Gate, on an outdoor stage
at the San Francisco Blues Festival,
lets loose a series of shrieks

and animal groans from deep in the jungle
of her great heart, drums and upright
bass keeping time behind something
older, more essential, than words.

And suddenly an enormous spiraling cloud
of seagulls descends from a clear sky.
White wings quivering with sunlight,
they tattoo the air with their answering cries.

LITTLE ELEGY

i.m. Vassar Miller, American poet, 1924--1998

Let us go down
to the stark Eden
of our deaths, that
grim paradise,
having truly lived.

May the wind in our bones
recognize the place,
asking nothing of God
but the chance to rest
there awhile; perhaps
just long enough
to remember you.

Part Two

THE ONSET

OF SOMETHING OMINOUS

CHINESE NEW YEAR, THE BOWERY

For Raymond Shen

Sometimes I can still see the dragon's
sequined, snapping jaws, the pale ribbon
of his body winding through swarming streets
where the dancers' footprints turn to smoke.

We kneel on a littered stoop, loading our cameras;
the smell of gunpowder clings to our hair and clothes.
A blizzard of burnt paper drifts over dreaming winos,
shopkeepers setting out spices for the bodiless dead.

CROSSING LARKSPUR FERRY

"Flood-tide below me! I see you face to face!"
  —Walt Whitman

Kneeling beside me, Mark tries in vain
to light a cigarette in strong wind, pointedly
ignoring the No Smoking sign posted nearby;
cursing under his breath as the flame goes out.

We rumble past Alcatraz, where birds nest
in the abandoned guard towers; past Angel
Island's unpeopled flanks; past the Marin
Headlands, already darkly mantled in mist.

Everything stands out sharply, as it does in dreams;
the light is what a friend in New York would call
mescaline light. Mark begins to reminisce about
Back East, where they have four distinct seasons.

He remembers when the Staten Island Ferry
was a "cheap date"; how twenty years ago,
he and Danny Ratcliff used to take their girls
out on the water, drunk on salt air and beer.

A little sadly, I realize we're no longer young—
somehow surprised by knowledge I bear daily now.
Times like these, when the weather's nearly perfect,
are rarer than they were; there's no doubt about it.

Nowadays, my life *weighs more* than it once did.
Something is bearing down on me, with a force
I'm helpless to resist. Mark feels it too, I know;
it passes unsaid between us, needing no words.

Rounding the point where San Quentin broods
like a medieval nightmare, we watch windsurfers
darting like dragonflies through the vessel's wake,
their transparent sails ethereal in a haze of spray.

One of them topples and goes down;
I think how we're always treading water,
every one of us, every day of our lives,
swept seaward by currents we can't control.

NIGHT BRACES

> "*Pain comes from the darkness,*
> *And we call it wisdom. It is pain.*"
> —Randall Jarrell

Adrift in the darkness of my fortieth year,
I feel again the heavy leather shoes
my father laced me into when I was four,
the way the gleaming metal braces
clicked into sockets in the heels.

How I cried out as he tightened the straps
that encircled each leg just below the knee,
until they blazed their angry alphabet into my skin,
years before the surgery had left its scars.

Long after his footsteps faded
the glass of water he left behind
glowed on the nightstand, lit
by a luminous shroud of sky
in the bedroom window.

Then I could feel a groan too faint for the ear,
the slow creak of tendons tightening on bone.

The stillness was broken twice an hour
by the mechanical cry of the cuckoo,
and sometimes by some farther bird
in whose inhuman trill I knew already
the pitiless insistence of pain.

THE CATHEDRAL

On the walk from the station,
heat climbs like smoke from empty plazas.
At the youth hostel, there are no vacancies.
I meet an Irishman named Ivan; ten dollars
between us, we decide to share a room nearby.

Ivan drinks red wine all night, talking loudly
about girls he's laid all across Europe.
By bad light, I eat a blood orange,
wrapping the rest in newspaper.

Before dawn, we set out
for the hill above town,
machine gun fire only blocks away.
The bus is packed with old women in black,
live chickens in wicker baskets.
It wobbles unsteadily down steep inclines,
narrow streets lined with shuttered houses.

Gaudi's unfinished masterpiece soars
like a drunken dream into a luminous sky.

In the roofless nave, the sun, already blistering,
beats down on columns like enormous trees.
Ivan takes a swig from a barely concealed bottle,
laughing wildly, his dark hair
flickering in the burning breeze.
Gargoyles leer from the parapets.
A cloud of dusty pigeons rises
through the empty rose window,
a host of derelict angels.
—*Barcelona, Summer, 1977*

THE PARTIAL HOSPITALIZATION UNIT
"I am, yet what I am, none cares or knows..."
—John Clare

In the library I unearth Sandburg's *Remembrance Rock,*
an anthology listing Yeats as a living poet, *Hungarian Cooking*.
Ours is an open ward, fairly quiet. But on the way to the restroom,
one must pass Intensive Care, its heavy steel door barred like a vault.
I can see nothing through the narrow window; I often hear screams,
sometimes sobbing—once, a sort of scraping sound I can't identify.

I do not sleep here. Every morning I arrive by streetcar.
On Mondays, we fill out lunch menus for the week.
It's always the same choices; the food, at least, is good.
None of the other patients speak as we unload our trays.
Usually, we eat in silence. The thin Salvadorian weeps softly.

For group therapy we arrange ourselves in a circle.
The social worker sits among us: plain, prim dress,
tight hair. Today the lesbian tells in a flinty voice
how her parents disowned her when she came out.
She doesn't like me, but nods when the Chinese kid

says he's been unable to leave his room for weeks.
Two hundred milligrams of Zoloft do nothing
to ease my growing sense of hopelessness.

Private sessions are even worse. When I tell the smug,
indifferent doctor in his tweed vest I'm still angry at a woman
who wrongfully accused me of harassment, his eyes narrow.
Do I know of the Terasoff Mandate, that he's required to warn
anyone I might intend to hurt? I insist I'm not violent,
but he isn't listening. He asks if I'm calmer on medication.
There's no point in bothering to answer.
—Langley Porter Psychiatric Institute, San Francisco, 1994

THE ONSET OF SOMETHING OMINOUS

Late afternoon, and the Pacific's a sheet
of burning metal wrinkling against the shore.
I stand for hours on the embankment
watching the sinking sun unraveling on the water.

Thoughts splinter like light among the froth and kelp.
Growing up with each step and gesture a struggle
hardens one too much to permit illusions: it isn't lust
or pity I wrestle with, but an encroaching grimness.

I'm thinking of a woman with Chinese writing
tattooed on the skin at the base of her neck.
I consider her now, not with longing,
but with something approaching despair.

High overhead, seagulls wheel
in torn circles through the twilight.
By the water's edge, the shadows
of the last birds shiver and take flight,

a flurry of wingbeats in the darkness.

I can still hear their departure
long after I no longer see them.
Night fills the emptiness they leave behind;
wind rattles the coarse grass of the dunes
as I turn and climb towards a sky without stars.

A LAMENT FOR MY FORTY-FOURTH YEAR

> "...lonely men in shirt-sleeves, leaning out of windows..."
> —T. S. Eliot

Already I imagine
I can see the beginnings
of the one I will someday become.
Old men on street corners
watch me with clouded eyes—
their slack faces fading
like the faces of statues
blurred by years of rain,
the blue hair of veins
leaking like languor
through their papery skin.

CATECHISM FOR A LEPER

> "The officiating priest threw a handful of earth from the cemetery on the head of the leper three times, explaining that the ritual symbolizes the death of the leper to the world."
> —*Saul Nathaniel Brody*, The Disease of the Soul

A Latin blessing trembles like the wind.
The priest explains the funeral is your own,
although for years to come you'll roam the world,
your eyes averted from the eyes of men,
your heavy footsteps like a tolling bell.

Feel the stench of graves anointing you:
decrepit earth, full of worm-stink and rot.
Know in your blindness that somewhere above,
the rose window is colorless and black,
empty at midnight as a gaping socket.

Attempt to concentrate on the only thing
you *can* see through the coarse cloth of your cowl:
the flames of candles on the distant altar,
cold and uncertain as the hope of Heaven,
like burning tears of an abandoned god.

Rise quietly, and quickly cross yourself
as you depart, your hood swept from your eyes.
Stand in the mossy portico among the saints,
the demons with their breasts of rain-dimmed stone,
their pity swallowed by the ravenous dark.

Then contemplate the road ahead of you:
a dusty torrent rushing toward a future
where Death awaits you with his arms outspread.
His emaciated body is your own:
a breathing corpse awash with running sores.

"Et mortua est in mundo, renascimur Deo."

THE TRUEST WORLD

The truest world is a vicious one,
whose nonchalant brutality
we glimpse only occasionally,
in moments of insight
that freeze the blood.

Today, for instance: high above
the "Hawks" logo on the retaining wall
reinforcing the hillside behind the playground,

I saw a real hawk—a silent, breathing crucifix
floating effortlessly in the overcast sky.

CIRO ON THE NIGHT BEFORE HIS WEDDING

I still remember his face,
younger than mine is now;
he sat in the flickering darkness,
arms folded on the steering wheel
of the tour bus, cigarette smoke
wreathing his head like a garnish
around the head of John the Baptist.

The marriage was arranged in the old way,
an alliance between families, a concept hard
for school kids from New Jersey to fathom:
he'd shrugged and told us (through an interpreter)
he didn't really know his future wife, had met her
once, maybe twice, didn't care, didn't really
think about it much one way or the other.

But I stayed behind while the others went
to climb the Spanish Steps, sitting with him
in the shadows, the idling engine tearing at silence,
no language flowering in the space between us.

I watched uneasily as composure was blown
from his features like dust from the surrounding ruins,
his dark eyes hardened by something more bitter
than sadness. We'd have another driver, I knew,
for the morning's trip south to the temples of Paestum.

—Rome, 1975

THE NUNS' MADHOUSE

> *"He heard a mad nun screaming in the nuns' madhouse beyond the wall."*
> —James Joyce

Here where it always seems to be night
they gather, wild-eyed, veins twitching
in their pinched, translucent faces.

Nurses move quietly among them,
melancholy angels carrying bedpans,
vials of blood bright as votive candles.

Above, in shadow, the body of Jesus
hangs like a limp sail from the mast
of a crucifix becalmed on the wall.

—*2006 version*

THE CEREMONY

There was a sweet smoke rising.
Silently and according to custom,
they washed the hair in urine,
sewed ears and nostrils shut,
stuffed the mouth with spices.
They dressed the infant's corpse
in an elaborate wedding gown,
determined to marry her
to the dead son of a prominent family
that she might not be lonely in paradise—
their own unspeakable grief woven
like river grass into her nuptial shroud.

The moon hung swollen and red.
Over the tiny bride they kept a vigil,
the silence pierced now and then
by the thin howl of a starving dog.

Near dawn, the ancestors
gathered just beyond the firelight:
tall, muscular folk with no faces,
sweat shining on their perfect limbs,
only darkness where their eyes should be.

THE LAST SHAKERS OF SABBATHDAY LAKE

"In the meetinghouse, we sit on plain benches. Walls are white, woodwork blue, the colors of light and sky."
—Richard and Joyce Wolkomir, "Living a Tradition,"
Smithsonian, *April, 2001*

Only eight still remain
of a sect which numbered
in the hundreds a century ago:
four men, four women, who sit
piously in the calm blue interior
of the meetinghouse, reading
aloud from an ancient Bible.

Through simple windows,
light falls into the thin white
hair of their bowed heads,
the camera making it look
(we must suspect deliberately)
almost as if they are haloed.

What's haunting in the photo
is what one hopes will endure
when they are gone: the honesty
of this room whose straight lines
lend it a kind of resolute dignity,
and of the altar, adorned plainly
with nothing but a wooden
bowl of perfect sunflowers.

NOTHING I LOVE HAS EVER SEEMED PERMANENT

For Pat

When I wake beside you the rags of summer sky
visible through partially drawn drapes are already
as thin and shimmering as blown glass. You're still
sleeping, sheets kicked away from your nakedness,
the curve of your shoulders traced faintly by the flicker
of the last streetlights. Propped on one elbow, I lie
watching for a long time as you curl more tightly into
some dream I can't share, smiling softly in your sleep.

At this hour loneliness is palpable even to lovers waking
in each other's arms. Across the way, by a cyclone fence,
the buses in the municipal yard doze in the intricate dark;
on the hill above them the neon sign over the storage facility,
partially burned out, prints the word *rage* in huge letters
on the waking world. The streets are wet, savagely quiet.

It's the most vulnerable time of day. Alone beside you here
in the fading shadows, I feel frail and old. There are some things
I fear: death, and the ordinary business of living. Nothing I love
has ever seemed permanent. I can scarce believe we're together
now, in this bed worn comfortable by the indentations of our bodies,
places where we fit gently into one another. Around us the new
day takes shape; the struggle begins. Frightened and joyous, let me
wake you with a kiss for luck, watching the rinsed light rise in your eyes.

TERRORS OF THE MILLENNIUM

> *"The pious were awaiting the coming of either the Redeemer or the Devil. The reason? The millennium was ending, and apocalypse seemed right around the corner."*
> —Smithsonian, July, 1999

Somewhere in Wales—let's say—
it's the end of the twentieth century.

Swallows nest in a ruined priory
while thunderheads gather in empty
windows, their *vitreaux* broken
by Henry's men, perhaps, or simply
crushed under the weight of centuries.

Foxglove and thistle push aside
tiles where a thousand years ago
the faithful lay prostrate: throngs
of penitents naked and bleeding
from hideous mortifications;
exhausted at the millennial hour;
throats hymned to hoarseness.

Those days are a distant echo,
a subtle dance of shadows only.
Their bones will not speak now;
they are no longer even dust.

The rain which begins, heavily,
is not a portent, neither brimstone
nor blood: it is rain. It falls as it must
on the oblivious hills, as the autumn night
settles over the drenched green world.

WALKING ACROSS THE SEA OF GALILEE

> *The Israeli government has approved plans to build a barely submerged foot bridge beneath the Sea of Galilee.*

Our aging guide moves with surprising agility.
Ahead of me two Serbian nuns struggle to keep
their balance on the submerged path, the hems
of their habits already soaked, brilliantly white
running shoes showing under dark, heavy skirts.

On either side of the narrow span, lifeguard stations,
uncomfortable-looking straight-backed chairs bolted
to wooden rafts, sway on chains furred with algae,
like tiny islands anchored deep in opaque water.

The lifeguards listen to Berlioz on a transistor radio.
Machine guns lie across their knees, gleaming dully;
sunlight slides easily off their bare brown shoulders.

Though the land's nearly two miles distant,
the scorched hills sharpen in the morning light.
There are no railings. We must walk carefully,
gingerly, arms outspread like awkward wings.

Yet it's easy to believe in this manufactured miracle.
We follow in the footsteps of Jesus towards the new
millennium, as the rattle of gunfire carries from shore:
wobbling across a wrinkled brown sea rank with salt,
each step uncertain enough to be an act of faith.

SUNRISE, SAN FRANCISCO, SEPTEMBER 1, 1999

> *"...As the clever hopes expire*
> *Of a low dishonest decade..."*
> —W. H. Auden, "September 1, 1939"

Here on the piers along the Embarcadero,
looking east to where the lights of Oakland
dim and vanish in the fog, we huddle together
on a wet bench, waiting for the mist to lift,
for a luminous pencil-thin line of light
to trace the jagged outline of the hills.

Holding you close, I'm surprised to think
of Auden's poem, sixty years old today,

another "low dishonest decade" gone,
a new millennium already looming.

The din of war is scarcely dimmer now;
the "error bred in the bone" dismays us still.

A metallic whine like an insect's
pierces the early morning quiet.
Not far from where we sit, a chopper
from the Naval Base on Treasure Island
hovers like a bee above shadowy waters,
bent on some errand we can only guess.
I hardly dare love you in such a world.

A new day sketches itself in around us,
swelling dawn's silhouettes with form and color.
The mist disperses as the burning arc of sun
lifts over the rim of night, beautiful and terrible,
a skirt of fire trailing a brilliant hem.

MORNING MEDITATION

For Rebecca Lyon

Inscribed on the rising mist, the pines
are characters in some strange alphabet
I've long ago forgotten how to read—
each branch a brushstroke placed deliberately,
spelling out something I seem meant to know:
a reassurance, or a call to praise.

One clear note shimmers and uncurls from
the lip of a delicate bell, shaped like a bowl,
a tone containing many tones within it,
its sound both simple and complex at once.
We close our eyes and concentrate on silence,
aware—for the first time—of our own breathing.

The farthest birdsongs sharpen and draw near.
Then, suddenly, the stillness is disturbed:
a wounded sound, like a suture being torn
from the air itself. I open my eyes to look
and glimpse a chicken hawk climbing to sunlight,
hauling a flurry of wingbeats after it.

THE YELLOW HOUSE IN ARLES

"Between two such beings as he and I," Gaugin reflected, "a sort of struggle was brewing."
—Joseph A. Harriss, "Strange Bedfellows," Smithsonian, *December, 2001*

Gaugin, in later years, described
Van Gogh when they shared
the house in Arles as *fou*—crazy—
telling anyone who would listen
how the distraught Dutchman
once ran half-naked and screaming
into the street after him, on a night
swarming with whirlpool stars.

That was also the night Vincent
amputated his ear with a razor,
presenting the grisly trophy
to a girl in the local brothel.

His 1888 rendering of the yellow house
with the scalloped fanlight over its green door
betrays the maelstrom raging within—
where Gaugin complained his friend
had reduced their life to perpetual squalor.

The walls are executed with frenzied brushstrokes;
we can almost feel the roughness of their stucco.
But it's the sky above that demands our attention:
deep cobalt blue, neither day nor truly night—
an empty sky: starless, Godless, utterly hopeless.

ELEGY WHICH SHOULD HAVE BEEN A BLUES

John Lee Hooker, 1917--2001

I met you years ago before a show,
waiting respectfully while you stood talking
to a young woman whose name was also Hooker,
who hailed from Mississippi as you did
and wondered whether you might be related.

Your speaking voice had in it all the grit
and anguish I'd admired on your records,
but there was an enormous dignity
about you no recording could convey.

By then you were a legend; even so,
when that young stranger introduced herself
you shook her hand and offered your own name,
as I imagined you'd been taught to do
when you were a child in the rural South.

IN RESPONSE TO A PREDICTION OF MY DEATH ON APRIL 4, 2031

> *"What instruments we have agree:*
> *The day of his death was a dark, cold day."*
> —W. H. Auden

A night just like tonight, perhaps; no moon,
only a few sullen clouds drifting languidly
towards the indifferent blister of the sunset,
the lights below them like embers in a fire.

I'll slip unnoticed from my wasted life,
the way a swimmer might discard a robe;
leaving behind me some few grieving friends;
sure, as I breathe my last, that I've been loved.

Should anyone miss me, let it be my wife;
and yet I'll leave the world with no regrets,
sure that the bond we share will last beyond
the narrow confines of our birth and death.

Then everything I was or might have been
will vanish into the realm of speculation:
nothing remaining of me but memories,
and some poetry no one will ever read.

A night just like tonight, or any other:
only a few dull clouds dispersing here
among the smoky tatters of the sky,
the city lights dissolving, and no stars.

WHO WANTS TO BE AN IMPOVERISHED POET?

Should you decide to devote your life to poetry,
you would most likely become which of the following?

Is it:

A. Famous, and wealthy beyond all dreams of avarice;
B. Known and respected among scholars and academics;
C. Broke and obscure, in a room that leaks when it rains;
or,
D. Dead before you reach the age of fifty?

Well, Regis, that would have to be A, wouldn't it?

Is that your final answer?

Part Three

THE ORDINARY

ARRIVAL OF DEATH

ELECTROCUTING THE ELEPHANT

Lulu's gone mad, but stubbornly refuses
to eat the poisoned carrots her keepers
have attempted to feed her; thus, another
means of dispatching her must be found.

It's 1904, a time when both
electrocution and moving pictures
are relatively recent developments,
and very much novelties,
so the execution is preserved
in grainy black and white.
(The electric chair, heralding
a flood of similar human deaths,
is still several years distant.)

The great beast kneels
on the floor of her cage
in the first throes of mute
uncomprehending agony
as the labyrinth of wires
crossing her broad back
crackles with the current—
searing her skin, spitting sparks
into the forest of coarse hair
along the ridge of her spine.
Seconds later, her dark bulk
topples, the life gone out of it.

Macabre as it seems, this grisly
event is destined to become
a popular feature in early cinemas.
The film is silent, of course.
In the background, the lights
of Coney Island flicker
like candles in a rising wind.

THE ORDINARY ARRIVAL OF DEATH

i.m. Marty Gordon

Cloudless sky, light like water on the street.

I'm depositing a check in an automatic teller when he
comes up behind me, grinning, removing his sunglasses,
amused by the lack of recognition, at first, in my eyes.

He stands smiling in the sun, handsome, young,
a shock of blond hair glowing on his forehead,
his face friendly, glad we've met—it's been years.
What do we talk about? An upcoming concert,
nothing much. "Nice to run into you again."

Later that night he's dead, fallen two stories
from an apartment balcony. Forgetting his key,
trying to climb in through a window, maybe drunk,
he lost his footing. I picture him grasping
at nothingness, spread on the air for an instant
as if in flight. And then darkness, nothing at all.

DROPPINGS

"My God! If I'm stuck in Oakland much longer, I'll wind up writing poems about pigeon shit!"
  —*Conversation with a friend*

In an empty city where enormous
buildings blacken a thin lavender sky,
great clouds of pigeons fill the bare
winter trees like feathered foliage,
a dark mass trembling with its own
breeze even on nights of no wind.

Sometimes, as though in response

to some silent signal, hundreds
rise together in shattered spirals,
a debris of oily feathers trailing behind;
as a burnt moon climbs through clouds,
their cooing blankets the sidewalks like a moan.

And sometimes, the strangest things
are suddenly—inexplicably—beautiful.
Beneath the pigeon trees, spattered droppings
shine on the asphalt in the failing light.

THE DOLLS

On Sutter Street, a row of Barbie dolls
is posed in sidewalk-level windows.
The old kind with real lashes blooming above
the perpetual astonishment in their eyes.
Their clothing is anything but innocent.
Studded leather, suggestive lingerie.
Ken sports a gold jumpsuit, clutches
a Gay Pride flag. A Black Barbie
strokes a ceramic kitten, an enormous
indolent tiger beneath her tiny hand.

It's a land of vixens and beasts. Each evening
I see them on my way home, speculate
about who collected them, arranged them
so lovingly on a dusty windowsill.
Then one night they're gone, the apartment
dark and empty. Painters' ladders and drop cloths
dimly visible through the glass.

Robert Lavett Smith

A STREET AT THE END OF THE WORLD

On the next corner, a forlorn little man
in a shabby Salvation Army uniform
plays the trumpet, a few coins shining dully
in his open case, like wishes in a fountain
long since gone dry. You're walking along alone,
stepping carefully over an iron grating where
the bad breath of the unseen subway rises
in a blur of heated steam. Ahead of you,
a crowd has gathered around a wooden crate
where a hustler deals cards.

                          And then it happens:
suddenly, and without warning, as you watch
his agile hands, you find you're thinking again
how flesh would burn free of the bone in seconds,
hustler and onlookers vaporized,
the street consumed in a roaring wall of flames.

And on a day just like today, perhaps:
the last sky you will ever see—this sky—
blue as a china plate about to break.
                  —Fourteenth Street, Greenwich Village, 1984

WATCHING THE TALL SHIPS

    For George R. Laurence

    "'Twas the night before OpSail,
    And all through the cliffs
    Not a camper was stirring..."
            —Campfire parody, 1976

The wrinkled Hudson far below us held
only the cobalt of the cloudless sky

and scattered fragments of midsummer light.
The breeze that stirred the trees around us made
the water's surface too rough for reflections;
but even so, the shadows of the sails
swelled and grew full upon the moving river.

Off to the east, the spires of Manhattan
rose gray and stony through the soot and smog;
the masts that swayed against their grimness seemed
like a young forest growing on the slopes
of jagged mountains, sheltered from the weather.

We'd made our camp atop the Palisades
the night before, and risen before dawn
to stake our claim to this bald bit of rock:
a windswept granite outcropping which gave
an unobstructed view downriver, towards
the harbor, towards the Verrazano Narrows
where the suspension bridge embraced the air
like a dull filament against the void.

George woke me earlier than I'd have liked.
Still groggy from a night of serious drinking,
we shaded our eyes and scanned the scene below;
the fierce glare from the water plunged its knives
into our brains, ripping our thoughts to shreds.

Now, the barque *Eagle* led the grand parade;
a swarm of smaller craft played in its wake,
while other tall ships slid in silhouette
beneath the bridge: schooners and Yankee clippers,
frigates, and whaling boats right out of Melville.
There must have been a hundred ships or more,
advancing with the splendor of a vision.

It was the summer before we left for college.

As always, George stood grinning at my side,
his boyish face flushed with enthusiasm,
his ginger hair already tinged with gray;
this was the summit of our innocence,
one fleeting moment when the future spread
before us like an endless possibility.

The years have run like water through my hands.
To say the world seemed *newer* then is wrong;
but when I think about that perfect dawn
high on the cliffs, it almost seems as though
I've lost the eye I once had for details.
Each line pulled taut against the shimmering sky,
each pole and spar, is burned into my mind
with a precision nothing since can match.

EINSTEIN THE WATCHMAKER

"If only I had known, I would have become a watchmaker."
—Albert Einstein, on his role in helping develop the atom bomb,
1955 (as quoted in Newsweek)

His wild hair brilliant by lamplight,
he squints through thick crystal
at the paper-thin gears his steady
hands place in their appointed
rounds, a well-ordered universe
being assembled on a tabletop.

It's already late. The tweezers
shine in his fingers like threads
of starlight. On nights like this,
he senses his destiny has always
had something to do with time,
although he sometimes wonders

whether it's really confined to

this tiny shop with its glittering
piles of stopped watches, its
ornate wooden cuckoo clocks
announcing each lonely hour
in a cacophony of song. It's

1955. The American invasion
of the Japanese mainland has
just ended, and with it, the last
vestige of the Second World War.
He is at peace tonight, except
for the recurring dreams which

have lately troubled him. Nightly, he sees
the world cleansed by a fire more horrible
than the fire of Malachi, millions of lives
vaporized in an instant. And at the boiling
center of the maelstrom, a voice repeating
gibberish, over and over: $E=mc^2$, $E=mc^2$....

COCKATOO AND COCKROACHES

For Victor Buxbaum

Grotesque as it seems, Pet World,
specializing in rare and unusual imports,
stocks a terrarium of Brazilian cockroaches
for the discriminating collector, shiny brown
wedges of life burrowing and scurrying
behind glass, flexing translucent wings.

There's also a cockatoo large as a cat,
brilliantly plumed in blue and gold,
but with a voice like something
in excruciating pain. It perches
on a swing in its huge cage, calmly
devouring the sign warning customers

not to get too close; repeated entreaties
produce nothing resembling human speech,
only a sort of sardonic chuckle
which sends a shiver through the afternoon.

MAXFIELD PARRISH

See especially "Daybreak" (1922)

He plumbed a past of his own making,
choosing for self-portrait the Pied Piper;
enchanting us all with luminous skies
piled high with magnificent clouds.

Yet he was modern, painting mostly
for calendars and advertisements,
a medievalist in an age
of mass production.

As the twenties roared around him
he must have endured their emptiness,
yearning for a time before skyscrapers,
telephones, motorcars, and aeroplanes.

You know his most famous print:
two young boys loiter in vined darkness
after a swim; one bends over his companion,
tempting him into the water behind them.

Beyond the shadowed colonnade
jagged hills glow with fantastic light;
the blue world bleeds gently to brown;
no sound disturbs the early morning quiet.

The lake is burnished bronze:
so still and starless it seems to hold,

like an echo or the end of a dream,
the image of the departed night sky.

THE SQUIRRELS
For Bob and Kathy De Luccia

As we lay sleepless, we could hear them gnawing
above us, in the attic unused for years.
Traps did no good: sprung at the oddest hours,
and always empty whenever we went to look.

At first, we just used salted peanuts for bait;
then almonds, walnuts, currants, and finally
dried figs as round and rich as silver dollars.
But nothing worked, and so the noise continued.

When spring came, they were noisier than ever,
their small sounds mingled with the dripping eaves;
all day their elusive scurrying dogged us like
the nagging memory of a childhood song.

We gave them names, beginning to suppose
we could distinguish the movements of each one
from among so many furtive rustlings, hearing
sounds faint enough to have been our imagination.

Then, more and more, we started to believe
that they resembled us, their features and habits
not so dissimilar from our own, although in fact
we'd never so much as caught a glimpse of them.

And when the wind was howling through the pipes
we knew the squirrels were talking to their dead.
One summer night we finally found one; mangled,
it had fallen down our chimney and broken its neck.

We grieved as we might have for a relative,
held a backyard funeral for the tiny corpse
with all the usual pomp and circumstance.
The others chattered overhead like ghosts.

FOR GEOFFREY HILL

"I will consider the outnumbering dead:
For they are the husks of what was rich seed."
    —G. H., *"Merlin," from* For The Unfallen (1959)

When the dead in Hell
gather together to drink
at their trough of blood
like flies at the throat
of a slaughtered bull,
their souls will be less
than the stench in the air,
their blathering blurred
to an inarticulate whine.

Your voice alone in that chorus of ghosts
will sing in finely wrought, still-human tones:
witnessing how, in a century seduced by death,
the rigors of language imposed a conscience
on the lubricious world, almost subduing
for a moment the obscenity of history.

THE DAY THEY CLOSED THE MUSTANG RANCH

"Sometime this summer, a bulldozer is supposed to
slam into the nation's first legal whorehouse."
    —San Francisco Chronicle, *April 23, 2003*

The low stuccoed building
broods in the desert sun.

At the cyclone fence by the main gate,
truckers from the interstate are turned away.

Sagebrush and memories remain;
miles of lonely Nevada highway.
A few of the girls linger in the parking lot,
in tight sequined dresses and short skirts,
their coats pulled close against a bitter wind.

No light penetrates the black-walled Dungeon Room,
where an enormous X sporting eyelets for chains
stands empty, its shackles dangling—
a vacant Cross awaiting a Savior.

SNOW ON THE COLORADO PLAINS

This late in the year a sudden thaw
seems to take the land by surprise:
the high, thin sky is achingly blue,
the weather so mild it could be
April instead of December.

But in places the shorn pastures
wear patches of unmelted snow,
where a tree's shadow or a boulder,
a stone wall or an abandoned barn,
has shielded the earth from sunlight.

Dulled to sepia by the dusty prairie wind,
these icy spots resemble the cloud shadows
one sometimes finds in old photographs;
they punctuate the surrounding landscape
like ominous pauses in conversation.

THE SONGWRITER ADDRESSES HIS FANS

"Prior to this lifetime
I surely was a tailor."
 —Paul Simon, "Fakin' It," from Bookends (1968)

His dark, intelligent eyes are shaded
by the brim of a Yankees cap he pushes
back only once, revealing for an instant
a head grown nearly bald.

Pale and small, he's almost a caricature,
the cadence of Queens still in his speech:
an aging tailor or grocer, whose hands
seem to cry *oy vey!* with every gesture.

Then he begins to sing. An instrumental track
pours pure exuberance from concealed speakers;
his voice is strong as he adds the unfinished lyric.

He seems to swell in stature as he sings;
and for a moment, he grows young.

BELL CHOIR

In the chancel
silver bells flare in the sun,
lips upward, like chalices.
When they're shaken
clear notes spill
from them like water.
Only music makes the world
bearable—music, and sometimes love.
Melody washes over us now
as we drink deeply
from the invisible
wine of gratitude.

A CYANIDE LAKE
IN AN OLD MINING TOWN

Victor, Colorado

A blue more faded than the frozen sky,
the water is the color of an eye—
blind and unblinking among the talus mounds,
it broods above the freight yards outside town:
too perfectly round for anyone to mistake
for either a sinkhole or a natural lake,
sheltered by slag heaps from the winter wind.

Here in the mountains, where the air is thinned,
the weak December sunlight seems to drain
down through the gravel filters like old rain,
as though the poisoned waters could extract
this metaphorical gold, as they in fact
once drew the true gold from the rock and rubble
back when the exhausted mine seemed worth the trouble.

EXPULSION FROM THE GARDEN

Porcelain plate, Italian, Urbino, mid sixteenth century

Once we were tenants of a fragrant Eden.
The world was new, both beautiful and terrible.
We were consumed by the terror and the glory,
like moths drawn near an incinerating flame
whose wings are charred until they match the darkness.

Who could have been content? We were invisible,
hidden in shadows we ourselves had cast:
the scant light of our lives was like the moon's
reflected glory, leaving us to doubt
whether the rumors we had heard were true
about a blazing radiance called *the sun*.

Now we awake to sunlight, blinking dumbly,
rubbing the sleep from eyes no longer blind,
and seeing the world at last for what it is:
not paradise, perhaps, but *ours*, and home.

AT YOUR BEDSIDE
For Pat, comatose following a hemorrhaged brain tumor

For more than four months now,
I have kept my bedside vigil, loving you,
fearing the world may prove unkind.

Your face is beautiful in sleep:
a placid mask beneath which
the dreams of your illness
lie gathered like embers—
a low, white heat unstirred
by morning's hand.

IN THE SHADOW OF THE REAPER
Site of the siege of Chartres, 1568

Beyond the walls, the failing light
falls on shorn fields lying fallow
in the husk of harvest, whispering
this emptiness was once an open grave.

Here, the bodies of the fallen festered,
stilled blood blackening their twisted limbs.
Beneath a ravenous cloud of flies, dead eyes
stared heavenward from splintered skulls.

Nothing remains of those heaped corpses now,
of the botched sacrifice's indecent meat:
the dull worm fattens on that glutted dust,
the bones have blurred into oblivion.

FLAMINGOES IN THE CAMARGUE

Having expected beauty,
a conflagration of plumage
igniting the sullen afternoon,
you're surprised by how ugly
they really are, how ordinary.

They rise in a dusty cloud,
faded feathers tinged with pink,
like cotton used to dress a wound.

There is nothing graceful
about their ungainly flight.

The dark water trembles,
but offers no reflection
of their passage.

PEPPERMINT PIG

At first glance, it appears
to be blown glass, or glazed
ceramic, a tiny figurine
so perfectly smooth
light drips off it like water.
The faintly pungent scent
of mint betrays it as candy,
its astonishing pink too hard
for the teeth. In certain families,
at Christmas, the peppermint pig
is broken for luck, shattered
by a blow from a hammer,
sweet fragments dissolving
like dreams on the tongue.
That's the way of it: luck,

when it finds us, arrives
in pieces, and we sift
through the rubble,
taking what we can.

INDEX OF TITLES

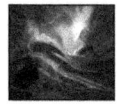

A Basket of Silk Flowers, *84*
A Cyanide Lake in an Old Mining Town, *199*
A Decorative Mantelpiece from Early in the Century, *124*
A Drunken Italian in a Bar in Milano Tries to Convince Me that I Am Christ, *14*
A Half-Empty Pack of Cigarettes, *126*
A Lament for My Forty-Fourth Year, *172*
A Letter to Meg in New York, *93*
A Nocturne for Fisherman's Wharf, *94*
A Palmistry, *71*
A Rural Staining, *3*
A Smell like Ashes, Guam, 1949, *40*
A Street at the End of the World, *190*
A Tricycle Abandoned on the Sidewalk after Dark, *104*
A Vietnamese Grass Beverage: Three Poems, *127*
After Brain Surgery, *157*
Among Believers, *111*
An African Carving, *123*
An Afternoon by the Carousel, *72*
An Old Man with an Easel, *35*
Ancestors, *18*
Answering the Riddle, *134*
Apple Trees, *133*
Ashtray, *8*
At a Civil War Reenactment, *86*
At Bean Hollow, *88*
At Last, like Sleepers, *159*
At the Fundamentalist Church, *74*
At Your Bedside, *200*

Attending the Bishop's Mass, 49
Audley End, 136
Bad Fruit, 107
Bell Choir, 198
Beyond Radio Range, 122
Bob Dylan Is Stopped by His Own Security, 160
Breviary, 4
Brie and Chianti at Midnight, 159
Buxtehude by Candlelight, 124
Catechism for a Leper, 172
Chinatown in Fog, 111
Chinese New Year, the Bowery, 167
Ciro on the Night before His Wedding, 174
Classical Musicians in the Subway, 158
Cockatoo and Cockroaches, 193
Cross of Nails, 38
Crosses Made of Flowers, 58
Crossing Larkspur Ferry, 167
Dana's Pipe, 95
Dance of the Dresses, 142
Deaf Woman Wrapping Christmas Gifts at Borders, 154
Dinner with Lisa, 59
Don't Look Now, 156
Dreaming in Black and White, 161
Dreaming of Aftershocks, 78
Driving Past, 104
Driving South from San Francisco, 42
Droppings, 188
Dust Bowl Funeral, 154
Earthquake Weather, 112
East of Modesto, 122
Einstein the Watchmaker, 192
Electrocuting the Elephant, 187
Elegy for a Spanish Poet, 43
Elegy Which Should Have Been a Blues, 182

Etta and the Seagulls, *162*
Even So, *52*
Expulsion from the Garden, *199*
Eyes, *16*
Falling out of Love at the Columbus Zoo, *60*
Family Chronicle, *62*
First Frost, *21*
Flamingoes in the Camargue, *201*
Fog on Ocean Beach, *104*
For Geoffrey Hill, *196*
For the Builder of Golden Gate Park, *97*
From One Who Has No Right to Grieve, *150*
From the 41st Floor, *95*
Gardening along the Fire Scars: Oakland, 1993, *155*
Goldilocks, *99*
Greetings from San Francisco, *27*
Hearses, *137*
History Rises, *50*
I Celebrate Five Years in San Francisco: October 6, 1992, *121*
I Die, *83*
If I Had My Druthers, *143*
Illinois Wedding, *79*
In an Antique Shop, *6*
In an Italian Restaurant, *5*
In Memory of a Failed Messiah, *75*
In Memory of Weldon Kees, *51*
In Response to a Prediction of My Death on April 4, 2031, *182*
In the Name of Science, *156*
In the Shadow of the Reaper, *200*
Jesus, *75*
Jesus in Bed between Us, *117*
Kickballs, *158*
Killing the Christmas Fly, *17*
Knife Grinder, *139*
Landscape with Figure, Standing Apart, *153*

Light and Darkness, 113
Little Elegy, 163
Loss, 49
Love Poem, 9
Lullaby and Dirge, 132
Maxfield Parrish, 194
Meatloaf, 114
Morning, 10
Morning Meditation, 180
My Father Emerges from the Depths, 81
My Father Takes Me Fishing, 120
My Grandfather's Vigil, 151
My Phantom Aunts, 3
New World, 27
New Year's Day: The Sutro Baths, 77
Nicollet in Wisconsin, 1639, 119
Night Braces, 168
Nocturne, 138
Nocturne for a Woman Nearing Middle Age, 13
Nothing I Love Has Ever Seemed Permanent, 177
October Moon, Nearly Full, through Clouds, 114
Omens and Portents, 55
On a Bus at Twilight, 29
Our High School Choir Performs at a Black Church, 82
Paestum, 40
Paterson, 82
Pebbles from a Northern Field, 115
Peppermint Pig, 201
Pictures of the Dead, 76
Pinocchio, 31
Portrait of a Lady, 34
Primer, 135
Rain Offshore, 107
Requiem, 44
Ruth in a Wheelbarrow, 30

Saint Jerome and the Skull, *61*
San Francisco, My Thirty-Fourth Year, *77*
Sand Dollars, *102*
Scène de Genre, *133*
Self Portrait at 34: On the Golden Gate Bridge, *72*
She Arrives Just at Dusk, *21*
She's Sure Her Hands Are on Fire, *16*
Simply Being Here, *108*
Snow in the Berkeley Hills, *98*
Snow on the Colorado Plains, *197*
Snow Watch, *11*
Some Kind of Permanence, *66*
Spring: Two Views, *73*
Sultan School for Handicapped Children, *58*
Sunday Morning, Early: The Richmond, San Francisco, *71*
Sunrise, San Francisco, September 1, 1999, *179*
Swimming off Bimini, Summer, 1965, *28*
Terri Arranges the Mantelpiece, *99*
Terrors of the Millennium, *177*
The Appian Way, 1974, *80*
The Blind Clarinet Player, *119*
The Blue Angels Pass Overhead, *87*
The Bo Tree, *65*
The Bodies of Bonnie and Clyde, *78*
The Book of Artichokes, *20*
The Bottlebrush Plant, *103*
The Brandenburg Concerti, *105*
The Bridge, Soon Afterwards, *87*
The Cathedral, *169*
The Ceremony, *175*
The Clockwork Farm, *152*
The Day They Closed the Mustang Ranch, *196*
The Death of Willie Dixon: As Reported on National Public Radio, January 29, 1992, *85*
The Death This Year, *56*

The Departure, 18
The Dolls, 189
The Dragon Robes, 12
The Dust Storm of April 14, 1935, 14
The Embarkation, 42
The Final Hours of the Twentieth Century, 150
The Flower Burning, 141
The Ghost in the Basilica, 46
The Glove Tree, 5
The Importance of Space, 100
The Last Shakers of Sabbathday Lake, 176
The Morning Mail, 117
The Nob Hill Mariners, 93
The Nun's Madhouse, 9
The Nuns' Madhouse, 175
The Onset of Something Ominous, 171
The Ordinary Arrival of Death, 188
The Partial Hospitalization Unit, 170
The Peacemakers, 136
The Pogo Stick, 45
The Rooms We Live In, 84
The Salt Shaker, 7
The Scrapbook, 118
The Seasons of a Year, 55
The Shave, 19
The Skull of Billy the Kid, 149
The Slow Loris, 101
The Songwriter Addresses His Fans, 198
The Squirrels, 195
The Stars, 54
The Trouble with the Garage Sale, 160
The Truest World, 173
The Unfinished Throne, 140
The Verrazano Narrows at a Distance, 38
The Visitors, 33

The Wedding, *131*
The Wedding Photographs of Strangers, *79*
The Werewolf's Grave, *57*
The White Peacock's Throat, *67*
The Windows, *48*
The Woman and the Orangutan, *15*
The Yellow House in Arles, *181*
Thirty Years after the War, *40*
Three Northern California Landscapes, *116*
Twilight, *Crème Caramel*, and a Woman Named Shawn, *83*
Unicorn Soup, *20*
Visiting the Undertaker, *35*
Waiting for the Thaw, *61*
Walking across the Sea of Galilee, *178*
Walking Alone at Night, *19*
Walking beside the Hudson, *63*
Watching a Blind Man in a Subway Station, *139*
Watching Marguerite, *32*
Watching the Tall Ships, *190*
Wedding: The Annunciation Greek Orthodox Church, Modesto, *125*
What the Eye Is Drawn To, *53*
Who Wants to Be an Impoverished Poet?, *183*
Why the French Seldom Eat Corn, *47*

ABOUT THE AUTHOR

R OBERT LAVETT SMITH lives in San Francisco. He holds a B.A in French from Oberlin College, where he also studied creative writing with Stuart Friebert and David Young, and an M.A. in English from the University of New Hampshire, studying with Charles Simic and Mekeel McBride. After graduating from UNH, he joined the Master Class at the 92nd Street YMHA in New York City, where he studied with Galway Kinnell. He has authored four small-press chapbooks (gathered here for the first time) and four previous full-length efforts, *Everything Moves With A Disfigured Grace*, *Smoke In Cold Weather: A Gathering of Sonnets*, *The Widower Considers Candles*, and *Sturgeon Moon*.

www.ingramcontent.com/pod-product-compliance
Lightning Source LLC
Chambersburg PA
CBHW020851090426
42736CB00008B/327